ECONOMIC ISSUES, PROBLEMS AND PERSPECTIVES

FOREIGN INVESTMENT IN THE U.S.

ECONOMIC ANALYSES AND SECURITY CONSIDERATIONS

ECONOMIC ISSUES, PROBLEMS AND PERSPECTIVES

Additional books in this series can be found on Nova's website under the Series tab.

Additional E-books in this series can be found on Nova's website under the E-book tab.

ECONOMIC ISSUES, PROBLEMS AND PERSPECTIVES

FOREIGN INVESTMENT IN THE U.S.

ECONOMIC ANALYSES AND SECURITY CONSIDERATIONS

THEODORE L. NEWELL
EDITOR

nova publishers
New York

For permission to use material from this book please contact us:
Telephone 631-231-7269; Fax 631-231-8175
Web Site: http://www.novapublishers.com

Additional color graphics may be available in the e-book version of this book.

Library of Congress Cataloging-in-Publication Data

ISBN: 978-1-62948-930-8

Published by Nova Science Publishers, Inc. † New York

CONTENTS

Preface		**vii**
Chapter 1	Foreign Direct Investment in the United States *Department of Commerce and the President's Council of Economic Advisors*	**1**
Chapter 2	Foreign Direct Investment in the United States: An Economic Analysis *James K. Jackson*	**17**
Chapter 3	Foreign Investment in the United States: Major Federal Statutory Restrictions *Michael V. Seitzinger*	**29**
Chapter 4	Foreign Investment and National Security: Economic Considerations *James K. Jackson*	**49**
Chapter 5	The Committee on Foreign Investment in the United States (CFIUS) *James K. Jackson*	**81**
Index		**123**

PREFACE

This book focuses on the foreign direct investment in the United States. It provides an economic analysis of foreign direct investment in the United States, discusses federal statutory restrictions, analyzes economic considerations on foreign investment and national security, and finally, focuses on the committee on foreign investment in the United States.

Chapter 1 - The United States has been the world's largest recipient of foreign direct investment (FDI) since 2006. Every day, foreign companies establish new operations in the United States or provide additional capital to established businesses. With the world's largest consumer market, skilled and productive workers, a highly innovative environment, appropriate legal protections, a predictable regulatory environment, and a growing energy sector, the United States offers an attractive investment climate for firms across the globe.

Chapter 2 - Foreign direct investment in the United States rebounded slowly after falling from the $310 billion recorded in 2008, a record surpassed only by the $320 billion invested in 2000 in U.S. businesses and real estate. According to preliminary data, foreign direct investment in the United States in 2012 fell from the amount recorded in 2011. (Note: The United States defines foreign direct investment as the ownership or control, directly or indirectly, by one foreign person [individual, branch, partnership, association, government, etc.] of 10% or more of the voting securities of an incorporated U.S. business enterprise or an equivalent interest in an unincorporated U.S. business enterprise (15 CFR §806.15 [a]). In 2011, according to U.S. Department of Commerce data, foreigners invested $234 billion in U.S. businesses and real estate. Foreign direct investments are highly sought after by many state and local governments that are struggling to create additional jobs in their localities. While some in Congress encourage such investment to offset the perceived negative economic effects of U.S. firms investing abroad, others are concerned about foreign acquisitions of U.S. firms that are considered essential to U.S. national and economic security.

Chapter 3 - Foreign investment in the United States is a matter of congressional concern. It is believed by some that the United States has an unusually liberal policy which allows foreigners to invest in virtually all American businesses and real estate and that these foreign investments undermine the American economy by making it vulnerable to foreign influence and domination. These critics argue that there is even foreign domination of some key defense-related industries and that the ability of the country to protect itself in a time of national emergency could greatly suffer. These critics further argue that extensive foreign investment in this country drives up prices which Americans have to pay for investments and, even more importantly, for houses and farmland in areas where there is a significant amount of foreign ownership.

However, others argue that the United States should welcome foreign investment because the influx of foreign money contributes to the creation of jobs in this country. Some also believe that the United States should be a kind of sanctuary for foreign money because of the political and economic instability which characterizes much of the rest of the world. It is also argued that, in this age of globalization of the world's economy, United States restrictions on foreign investment will only impair this nation's economy and cause us to appear isolationist.

This report takes a look at some of the major federal statutes which presently restrict investment by foreigners. The report first gives a brief history of foreign investment in the United States. It then reviews constitutional justifications and constitutional limitations which exist concerning federal statutory restrictions on foreign ownership of property. After that follows a discussion of some of the major federal statutes which limit foreign investment in the United States. Some of these statutes will be looked at in detail, but a detailed treatment of such other laws as the tax laws, the antitrust laws, and the immigration laws is beyond the scope of this report.

Chapter 4 - The United States is the largest foreign direct investor in the world and also the largest recipient of foreign direct investment. This dual role means that globalization, or the spread of economic activity by firms across national borders, has become a prominent feature of the U.S. economy and that through direct investment the U.S. economy has become highly enmeshed with the broader global economy. This also means that the United States has important economic, political, and social interests at stake in the development of international policies regarding direct investment. With some exceptions for national security, the United States has established domestic policies that treat foreign investors no less favorably than U.S. firms.

The terrorist attacks on the United States on September 11, 2001, spurred some Members of Congress and others to call for a reexamination of elements of the traditionally open environment in the United States for foreign investment. In particular, some Members argue that greater consideration must be given to the long-term impact of foreign direct investment on the structure and the industrial capacity of the economy and on the ability of the economy to meet the needs of U.S. defense and security interests. In addition, policymakers from a broad group of nations are evaluating their national policies concerning foreign investment within the context of their national security concerns. As a result of these initiatives, Members of Congress may be pressed to address U.S. policies that focus on the role of foreign direct investment more extensively within a broader national security framework.

This report assesses recent international developments as the leaders from a number of nations work to reach a consensus on an informal set of best practices regarding national restrictions on foreign investment for national security purposes. This report also provides one possible approach for assessing the costs and benefits involved in using national policies to direct or to restrict foreign direct investment for national security reasons. Within the United States, there is no consensus yet among Members of Congress or between the Congress and the Administration over a working set of parameters that establishes a functional definition of the national economic security implications of foreign direct investment. In part, this issue reflects differing assessments of the economic impact of foreign investment on the U.S. economy and differing political and philosophical convictions among Members and between the Congress and the Administration.

Chapter 5 - The Committee on Foreign Investment in the United States (CFIUS) is comprised of nine members, two ex officio members, and other members as appointed by the President representing major departments and agencies within the federal executive branch. While the group generally has operated in relative obscurity, the proposed acquisition of commercial operations at six U.S. ports by Dubai Ports World in 2006 placed the group's operations under intense scrutiny by Members of Congress and the public. Prompted by this case, some Members of the 109th and 110th Congresses questioned the ability of Congress to exercise its oversight responsibilities given the general view that CFIUS's operations lack transparency. Other

Members revisited concerns about the linkage between national security and the role of foreign investment in the U.S. economy. Some Members of Congress and others argued that the nation's security and economic concerns have changed since the September 11, 2001, terrorist attacks and that these concerns were not being reflected sufficiently in the Committee's deliberations. In addition, anecdotal evidence seemed to indicate that the CFIUS process was not market neutral. Instead, a CFIUS investigation of an investment transaction may have been perceived by some firms and by some in the financial markets as a negative factor that added to uncertainty and may have spurred firms to engage in behavior that may not have been optimal for the economy as a whole. In the 112th Congress, some Members expressed their concerns to the Obama Administration over the national security implications of a proposed acquisition of a U.S. technology company by the Chinese-owned Huawei Technologies.

In the first session of the 110th Congress, the House and Senate adopted S. 1610, the Foreign Investment and National Security Act (FINSA) of 2007. On July 11, 2007, the measure was sent to President Bush, who signed it on July 26, 2007. It is designated as P.L. 110-49. On January 23, 2008, President Bush issued Executive Order 13456 implementing the law. The Executive Order also established some caveats that may affect the way in which the law is implemented. These caveats stipulate that the President will provide information that is required under the law as long as it is "consistent" with the President's authority "to (i) conduct the foreign affairs of the United States; (ii) withhold information the disclosure of which could impair the foreign relations, the national security, the deliberative processes of the Executive, or the performance of the Executive's constitutional duties; (iii) recommend for congressional consideration such measures as the President may judge necessary and expedient; and (iv) supervise the unitary executive branch." Despite the relatively recent passage of the amendments, some Members of Congress and others have questioned the performance of CFIUS and the way the Committee reviews cases involving foreign governments, particularly with the emergence of direct investments through sovereign wealth funds (SWFs). The Obama Administration issued a statement on June 30, 2011, supporting an open investment policy, a commitment to treat all investors in a fair and equitable manner, and support for business investment from sources both home and abroad in the economy. On September 28, 2012, President Obama used the authority granted to him under FINSA to block a Chinese acquisition of a U.S. energy firm.

In: Foreign Investment in the U.S.
Editor: Theodore L. Newell
ISBN: 978-1-62948-930-8

Chapter 1

FOREIGN DIRECT INVESTMENT IN THE UNITED STATES*

Department of Commerce and the President's Council of Economic Advisors

EXECUTIVE SUMMARY

The United States has been the world's largest recipient of **foreign direct investment (FDI)** since 2006. Every day, foreign companies establish new operations in the United States or provide additional capital to established businesses. With the world's largest consumer market, skilled and productive workers, a highly innovative environment, appropriate legal protections, a predictable regulatory environment, and a growing energy sector, the United States offers an attractive investment climate for firms across the globe.

Foreign Direct Investment in the United States Is Substantial

- In 2012, net U.S. assets of foreign affiliates totaled $3.9 trillion. The United States consistently ranks as one of the top destinations in the world for foreign direct investment (FDI), with inflows totaling $1.5

* This is an edited, reformatted and augmented version of the Council of Economic Advisors, dated October 2013.

trillion in FDI just since 2006. For 2012, FDI inflows totaled $166 billion.

- The U.S. manufacturing sector draws a considerable share of FDI dollars, led by pharmaceuticals and petroleum and coal products. Outside manufacturing, wholesale trade; mining; non-bank holding companies; finance and insurance; and banking receive the greatest shares of foreign investment.
- Investment flows into the United States come mostly from a small number of industrial countries. Since 2010, Japan, Canada, Australia, Korea, and seven European countries[1] collectively have accounted for more than 80 percent of new FDI. Although still small, flows from emerging economies like China and Brazil are growing rapidly.

Foreign Direct Investment Benefits the U.S. Economy

- In 2011, value-added by majority-owned U.S. affiliates of foreign companies accounted for 4.7 percent of total U.S. private output.
- These firms employed 5.6 million people in the United States, or 4.1 percent of private-sector employment. About one-third of jobs at U.S. affiliates are in the manufacturing sector.
- These affiliates account for 9.6 percent of U.S. private investment and 15.9 percent of U.S. private research and development spending.
- In the 2008-09 recession and subsequent recovery, employment at U.S. affiliates was more stable than overall private-sector employment. As a result, U.S. affiliates' share of total U.S. manufacturing employment rose from 14.8 percent in 2007 to 17.8 percent in 2011.
- Compensation at U.S. affiliates has been consistently higher than the U.S. average over time, and the differential holds for both manufacturing and non-manufacturing jobs.

Looking ahead, the United States will remain an attractive destination for foreign investment, and this investment will help bolster our economy. However, we need to continue to nurture and build upon the underlying strengths of the U.S. economy that make firms want to invest here; including an open investment regime, a large economy, a skilled labor force, community colleges, world-class research universities, predictable and stable regulatory regime, adequate infrastructure, and new energy sources.

Foreign Direct Investment in the United States

Every day, foreign companies establish new operations in United States or provide additional capital to established businesses. The United States consistently ranks as one of the top destinations in the world for this foreign direct investment (FDI) and has been the largest recipient of FDI since 2006, with investments totaling more than $1.5 trillion.[2]

This investment strengthens our economy by supporting good-paying jobs for millions of American workers, expanding our exports, and funding research and development. This paper reviews the factors that individually and collectively make the United States a sought-after destination for foreign investment, examines recent trends in FDI, and outlines benefits from FDI for the entire economy.

IN-SOURCING: THE DOMESTIC EQUIVALENT OF FDI?

There has been much interest recently in the phenomenon of "in-sourcing," which describes decisions by U.S.-owned firms to move certain of their operations back from abroad. While this is not FDI into the United States (because the investor is not foreign), in-sourcing decisions are motivated by many of the same considerations that motivate FDI.

The 2013 Economic Report of the President contains a detailed discussion of in-sourcing that includes the role of our productive workers, highly innovative environment, appropriate legal protections, and growing energy sector in attracting investment by U.S. firms back to the United States. That discussion also explains the concept of hidden costs. These matter also for FDI but are very concretely grasped in the context of in-sourcing.

In earlier decisions to locate abroad, many U.S. firms may have been motivated by a quest to pay low wages, but may not have had a full picture of the productivity drag that they would bear because of less productive workers, inadequate legal protections, and a generally more risky environment. As these costs became apparent, some firms moved operations back.

Distance itself can be costly. Compared with operating in the United States, setting up a supply chain far away and learning to communicate with suppliers requires many long trips and much time of top executives—time that could be spent on introducing new products or processes at home.

There is also greater risk from a long supply chain, because shipping prices and delivery times can vary enormously. In addition, U.S. companies are coming to value more highly the advantages that come from having production, innovation, and design close together. For example, the experience of manufacturing often motivates ideas for new products. Thus, Intel manufactures its most advanced chips in the United States, near where they are designed. Some in-sourcing clearly traces to a greater recognition of the benefit that comes from recognizing and avoiding these costs, and a desire to capture that benefit.

Drivers of Foreign Direct Investment in the United States

The U.S. is increasingly attractive as a destination for business investment, including FDI, for many reasons and companies and experts from around the world agree. In its June 2013 FDI Confidence Index, the U.S. surged past countries like China, Brazil and India to become the country with the top FDI prospects globally, as ranked by 302 companies representing 28 countries and multiple industry sectors. 2013 marks the first time that the US occupies the #1 spot in the survey since 2001. No single factor explains why the United States is an attractive destination for investment. This discussion highlights a few, and the way they interact:

- An open investment regime
- A large economy with big and diverse consumer markets
- A skilled labor force
- Community colleges, incorporating skill-development missions
- The world's top research universities
- Predictable and stable regulatory regime, including appropriate intellectual property protections
- Adequately capacitated infrastructure
- New sources of energy

For decades, and across presidential administrations, the United States has upheld an open investment policy, which affords companies national treatment regardless of country of origin. President Obama reaffirmed the U.S. commitment to an Open Investment Policy in 2011. A recent study finds that access to markets is one of the factors that significantly affect the decisions of multinationals to locate in the United States.[3] For example, a policy of "build where you sell" allows firms to gain deep insight into how local consumers use a firm's product, uses that may differ significantly from in a multinational's home market. In our bilateral investment treaties (BIT), national treatment is a core obligation that ensures that investors and investments receive treatment no less favorable than each treaty party accords to its own investors and investments within its own territory.

The U.S. economy is the largest in the world, and with median household income of $51,017, offers a large and steady demand for a variety of products.[4] The workforce is highly skilled and innovative. Our business regulations are among the most transparent and least cumbersome, including appropriate intellectual property protections. Exporting from the United States is relatively easy and inexpensive.[5] To these long-standing American strengths, we add the more recent increases in energy availability and decreases in energy costs.[6]

In the past, low wages and cost competitiveness were considered synonymous, with businesses "chasing low wages" with an eye on achieving cost savings, regardless skill and productivity differences between the low-wage and American workforces. However, experience in low-wage countries has given businesses a more nuanced point of view, especially as wage inflation in some countries has exceeded productivity growth. Put another way, businesses have learned that today's low wages may be gone tomorrow and that other costs and risks can offset the savings from cheap labor.

The United States' strong community college system increasingly emphasizes industry-focused training for high-demand occupations, with those efforts bolstered by various Administration efforts to ensure the availability of skilled workers for all firms operating in the United States. Our research universities are top ranked (15 of the top 20 universities in the world are located here); they are essential partners for companies making R&D investments here. The United States sits among the top five of the World Intellectual Property Organization's rankings in both investment in knowledge as a share of GDP and innovation.[7]

Those investments further benefit from the world's best intellectual property (IP) protection regime.[8] Government fees for obtaining a U.S. patent are among the lowest in the industrialized world.[9,10] Appropriate trademark protections protect companies' investments in brand and reputation. The U.S. Patent and Trademark Office bolsters those protections by performing "relative grounds examination" of trademark applications, ensuring that potential trademarks are not likely to be confused with currently active, registered trademarks. This up-front vetting of a brand or mark guards against potentially costly trademark disputes in the future. These protections benefit the owners of the IP and may benefit the United States as a whole. Empirical evidence points to a positive correlation between such protection of IP and economic growth.[11] This appropriate IP regime is just one example of the stable and predictable regulatory environment that the United States has on offer. This makes doing business easier. In 2013, the World Bank ranked the United States fourth out of 185 countries in terms of the "ease of doing business."

Also important to the ease of doing business is the ability to move goods and services around. Although U.S. infrastructure would benefit from significant investment, as the President has proposed, the United States does have world class ports plus a freight rail, air transportation, and a road network that are capable of not only serving the large U.S. market but making the United States a base for exports as well.

Increased domestic energy production has brought down prices and brightened the energy outlook, most notably for natural gas. Between 2007 and 2012, U.S. prices dropped nearly 60 percent as production rose and new reserves were uncovered. The country's natural gas boom has catalyzed domestic and foreign investment in petrochemical manufacturing as well as in the manufacturing of steel and equipment needed for gas extraction. Multiple industries benefit directly from inexpensive U.S.-produced natural gas because of its diverse industrial uses, ranging from on-site electricity generation to process heating, space heating, steam generation, and petrochemical processing. In addition, rapidly growing demand for renewable energy offers opportunities for firms to produce domestically in order to offset high shipping costs for heavy parts such as wind turbine towers and blades.

There Is Already Substantial Foreign Direct Investment in the United States

In 2012, the foreign investment position, or stock of foreign investment, in the United States was $3.9 trillion (at market value), including new inflows of $166 billion[12]. Inflows fluctuate broadly from year to year, with large drops in FDI flows roughly coincident with global recession years and relatively slow growth in FDI flows in the years immediately following.[13] Since 1997, the inflows reached a peak of $321 billion in 2000, coinciding with a peak in the business cycle, before falling to a low of $64 billion in 2003. Investment flows climbed in the subsequent economic expansion to a high of $310 billion in 2008. In 2009, FDI inflows dropped to $150 billion, rebounded in the next two years, and then edged down to $166 billion in 2012.

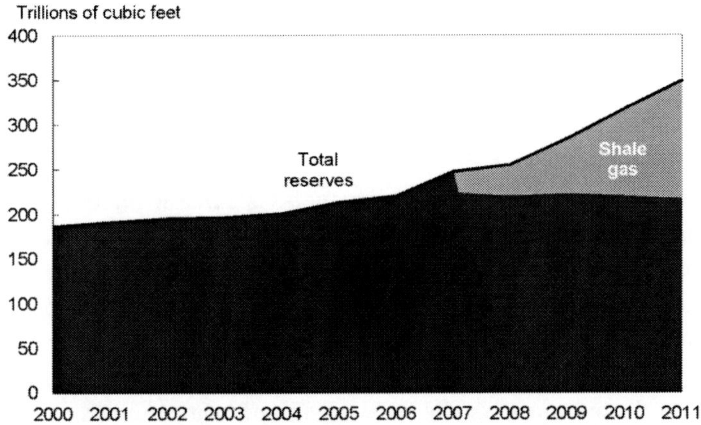

Source: Department of Energy, Energy Information Administration.

Note: The energy Information Administration began to collect separate estimates of shale gas reserves in 2007.

Figure 1. U.S. Natural Gas Proved Reserves, 2000-2011.

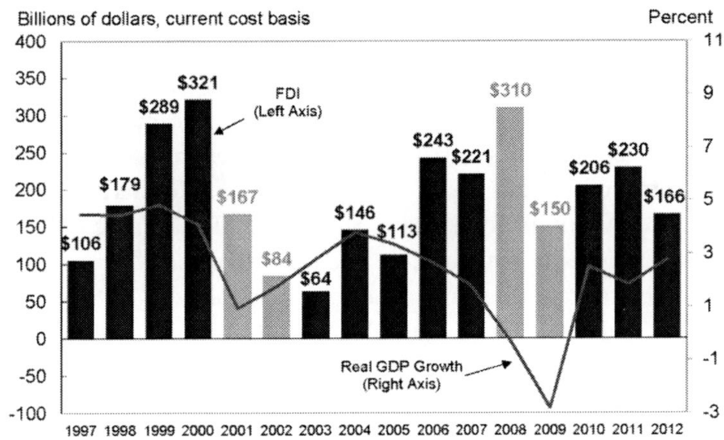

Source: Department of Commerce, Bueau of Economic Analysis; International Monetary Fund.

Note: Light blue shading denotes a global recession year (real GDP growth was below 3 percent).

Figure 2. Foreign Direct Investment in the U.S. 1997-2012.

Investment flows into the United States come mostly from a small number of industrial countries. From 2010 to 2012 (roughly -- the current expansion), Japan, Canada, Australia, and seven European countries collectively accounted for 83.5 percent of FDI inflows to the United States.[14] Companies from the United Kingdom have been the biggest recent investors, accounting for 17.1 percent of FDI inflows from 2010 to 2012. Switzerland is the second biggest source of FDI, with 10.6 percent of FDI inflows, largely concentrated in chemicals, followed by 9.7 percent from Luxembourg, concentrated in the finance and insurance industries.

Investment inflows from emerging markets remain relatively small. For example, FDI from China averaged slightly less than $1 billion in 2010-2012, or 0.5 percent of total FDI into the U.S, while inflows from Brazil averaged $1.9 billion, or 1.0 percent of the total. But these investments from emerging nations mark a dramatic increase from the negligible levels a decade earlier. Historically, investment from emerging nations into the United States has been hindered by factors such as the lack of financial resources, uncompetitive products for the U.S. market, unfamiliarity with the U.S. market, and low labor costs at home. Many of these factors are changing. Some emerging economies, such as China, Taiwan, and Brazil, have accumulated large foreign exchange reserves through trade surpluses. For many companies in these countries, financing investment projects abroad is becoming easier, and some of these companies have acquired the size, expertise, and networks to compete worldwide. Rising wages associated with economic development in these countries has narrowed wage gaps with the United States. This narrowing, along with high U.S. labor productivity and market-friendly features of the United States, makes undertaking new investment here an attractive option.

The U.S. manufacturing sector draws a considerable share of FDI dollars. Over the last ten years, manufacturing's share of FDI averaged 39.2 percent, and has increased to 45.4 percent in the last two years. From 2010-2012, pharmaceuticals accounted for nearly one-quarter (23.6 percent) of manufacturing FDI, followed by petroleum and coal products (16.5 percent); electrical equipment, appliances, and components industry (9.6 percent); basic chemicals (9.0 percent), and transportation equipment (9.0 percent). A look under the hood finds that the transportation equipment investments were mostly in the motor vehicle industry; German investors funded one-third of such inflows, and Japanese investors one-fifth.

Aside from manufacturing, sectors that received significant FDI from 2010-2012 were wholesale trade (11.1 percent of total FDI), mining (10.7 percent), non-bank holding companies (10.6 percent), finance (except banking) and insurance (7.8 percent), and banking (6.4 percent).[15] Between 2009 and 2011 outflows of investment from the United States information sector exceeded inflows, leading to some net disinvestment in that sector. However, net investment flows turned positive again in 2012. About 5 percent of the foreign investment position (or net financial claims) are in this industry.

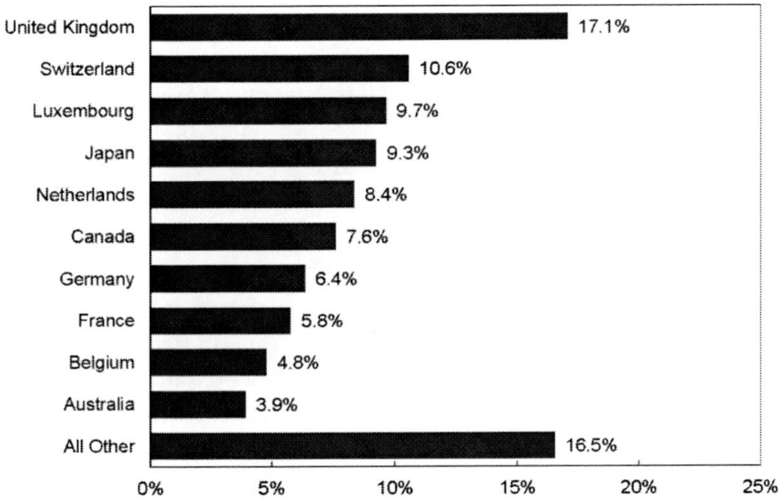

Source: Department of Commerce, Bureau of Economic Analysis.

Figure 3. Foreign Direct Investment into the U.S. Top 10 Investor Countries, 2010-2012 Average.

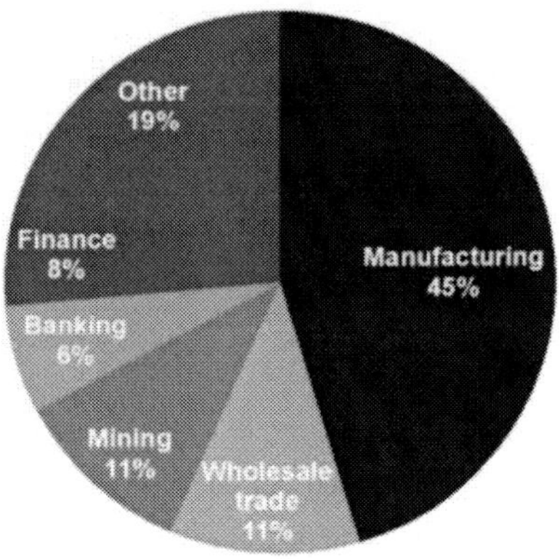

Source: Department of Commerce, Bureau of Economic Analysis.

Figure 4. Foreign Direct Investment into the U.S. by Industry Percent of Total, 2010-2012.

Foreign Direct Investment Benefits the U.S. Economy

Inbound foreign direct investment funds a number of physical assets, including production plants, research and development (R&D) facilities, sales offices, warehouses, and service centers. It can take the form of a "greenfield" establishment that creates something from scratch or a merger or acquisition ("M&A") of a sufficiently large stake in an existing enterprise. Whatever the form, it ultimately translates into output, jobs, exports, and R&D on American soil—data on which are captured in the Bureau of Economic Analysis' operations statistics on majority-owned U.S. affiliates of foreign firms. The vast majority of U.S. affiliates of foreign firms involve at least a 50 percent foreign ownership stake, and BEA publishes its most detailed operational data on these "majority owned" firms, which will be referred to as U.S. affiliates of multinational companies or "affiliates" from here on.[16]

Between 2010 and 2011, the value-added production of affiliates rose 11.4 percent to $736 billion. This output accounted for 4.7 percent of total U.S. private output. These firms employed 5.6 million people in the United States, or 4.1 percent of private sector employment. Consistent with estimates of the investment position by industry, about one-third of jobs at U.S. affiliates are in the manufacturing sector.[17] Manufacturing employment at U.S. affiliates was 2.1 million in 2011, or 17.8 percent of all U.S. manufacturing employment. Next to manufacturing, the largest industry sectors for employment by U.S. affiliates are wholesale trade, which employed 546,600 workers in 2011; retail trade with 488,500; and administration, support, and waste management, with 482,200.

In the 2009-09 recession and subsequent recovery, employment at U.S. affiliates proved more stable than overall private-sector employment. Total affiliate employment increased by 0.9 percent between 2007 and 2011, while total U.S. private employment fell 5.3 percent. Likewise, employment at manufacturing affiliates edged down just 1.5 percent from 2007 to 2011, compared to a 15.4-percent drop in overall U.S. manufacturing employment. As a result, U.S. affiliates' share of total U.S. manufacturing employment rose from 14.8 percent in 2007 to 17.8 percent in 2011.

U.S. affiliate firms make substantial investments in capital equipment and R&D, tend to hire highly skilled workers and pay excellent wages. These firms paid wages and other forms of compensation that averaged more than $77,000 per U.S. employee in 2011 as compared to average earnings of $58,000 for workers in the economy as a whole. Compensation at U.S. affiliates has been consistently higher than the U.S. average over time, and the differential holds for both manufacturing and non-manufacturing jobs, with a slightly higher differential in manufacturing.

DATA ON FOREIGN DIRECT INVESTMENT IN THE UNITED STATES[1]

Data in this report are from the Bureau of Economic Analysis (BEA) unless otherwise noted. BEA collects two broad sets of data on foreign direct investment in the United States: (1) international transactions (balance of payments) and direct investment position data, and (2) financial and operating data of U.S. affiliates. Each of these data sets focuses on a distinct aspect of foreign direct investment. The financial and operating data provide a picture of the overall activities of the U.S. affiliates, and the international transactions and direct investment position data cover foreign investors' transactions with, and position in, both new and existing U.S. affiliates.

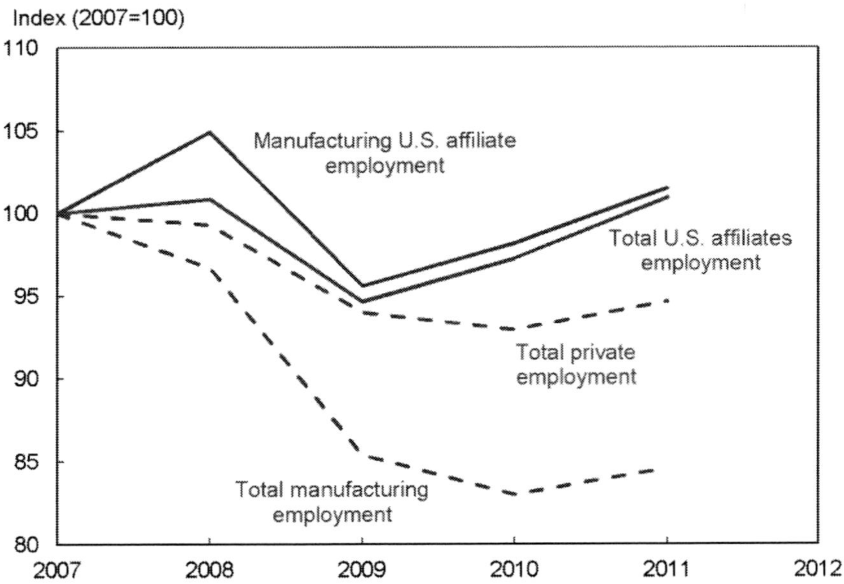

Source: Department of Commerce, Bureau of Economic Analysis.

Figure 5. Employment, 2007-2011.

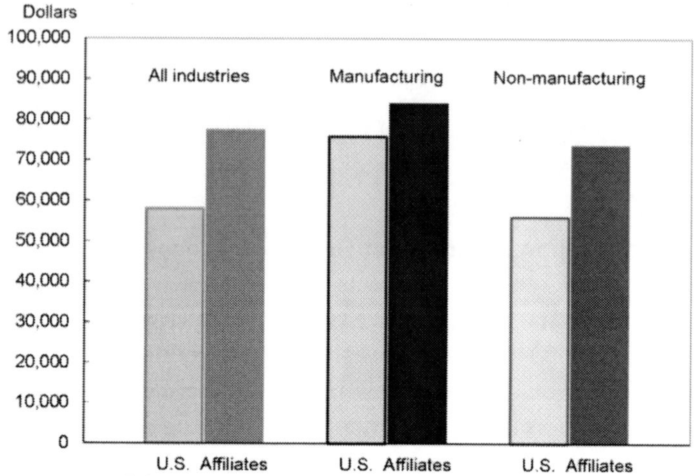

Source: Department of Commerce, Bureau of Economic Analysis.

Figure 6. Annual Compensation per Employee, 2011.

More generally, the U.S. affiliates are typically high-productivity firms that are major private-sector contributors to efforts to innovate and build. U.S. affiliates contribute 9.6 percent of total U.S. private investment and 15.9 percent of total U.S. private R&D. U.S. affiliates are also well-integrated globally and are the source of 20.5 percent of total U.S. goods exports.

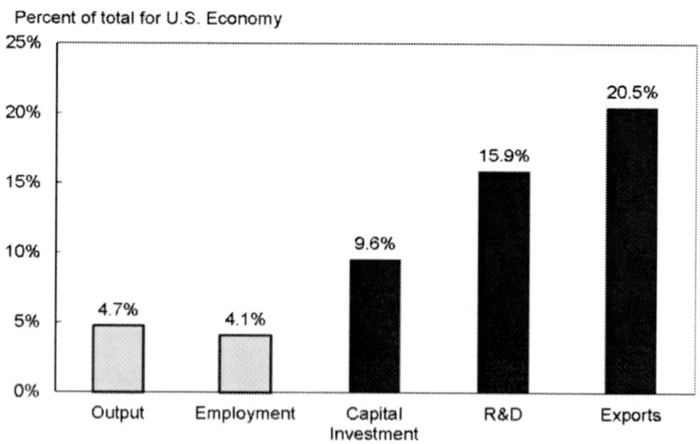

Source: Department of Commerce, Bureau of Economic Analysis; National Science Foundation.

Figure 7. Economic Activities of Majority-Owned U.S. Affiliates of Foreign Companies, 2011.

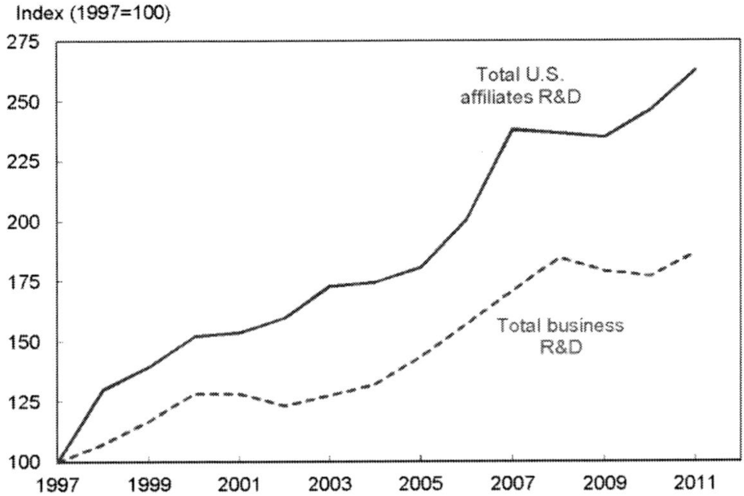

Source: Department of Commerce, Bureau of Economic, Analysis; National Science Foundation Note: Prior to 2007, FDI data do not include U.S. affiliates of foreign banks.

Figure 8. R&D Expenditures, 1997-2011.

A second positive benefit of U.S. affiliates is their high research and development (R&D) spending. U.S. affiliates account for a rising amount and share of U.S. businesses' research and development expenditures. In 2011, these firms spent $45.2 billion on R&D, accounting for 15.9 percent of total R&D spending by businesses.[18] Since 1997, when the data were first published, R&D expenditures of U.S. affiliates have climbed 163 percent, close to double the 87 percent growth among overall business spending on R&D.

The bulk of the R&D investments were in the manufacturing sector, with the manufacturing sector accounting for 69.9 percent of total R&D expenditures by U.S. affiliates, nearly equal to the 68.5 percent manufacturing share of business R&D spending across all firms. Affiliates in the wholesale trade sector spent $7.0 billion on R&D in 2011,[19] followed by the professional, scientific, and technical services sector ($4.1 billion), and the information sector ($1.5 billion).

In 2011, the majority of R&D expenditures by U.S. affiliates were from the top investor countries – specifically, Switzerland, the United Kingdom, Japan, France, and Germany. Swiss-owned affiliates have spent the most of any country on R&D since 2009, holding steady at approximately $9.0 billion annually during that time.

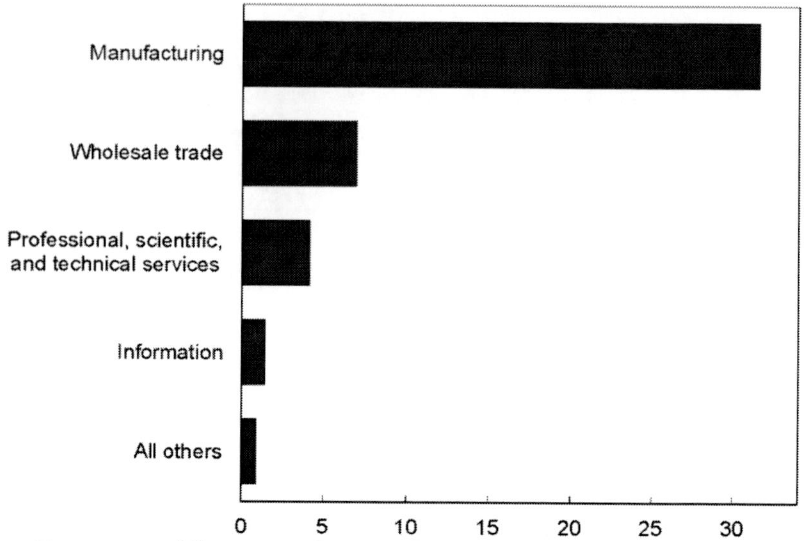

Source: Department of Commerce, Bureau of Economic Analyis.

Figure 9. R&D Expenditures by U.S. Majority-Owned Affiliates Billions of Dollars, 2011.

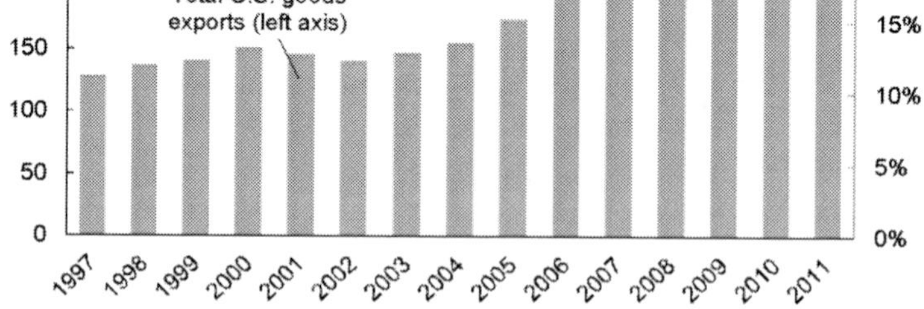

Source: Department of Commerce, Bureau of Economic Analysis.
Note: Data prior to 2007 do not include U.S. affiliates of foreign banks.

Figure 10. Exports of Goods by Majority-owned U.S. Affiliates of Foreign Firms, 1997-2011.

Finally, U.S. affiliates of foreign firms account for a disproportionate share of total U.S. exports (relative to their employment size). In 2011, U.S. affiliates exported $303.7 billion of goods, accounting for 20.5 percent of total U.S. exports, the second highest share since 1995. As the chart highlights, goods exported by U.S. affiliates follow the broad trends of overall exports, but tend to do better during economic downturns, likely because U.S. affiliates tend to trade heavily with their parent group and related parties, such as subsidiaries, foreign affiliates and sister companies. In fact, a significant portion of their exports – 59.0 percent in 2011 – is classified as a related-party transaction. This share of transactions has been constant throughout the time period and remains an important source of overall exports. These firms are heavy importers of goods as well, accounting for 28.4 percent of total U.S. imports—contributing to our negative trade balance but also further illustrating how these firms link the United States to the global economy.

CONCLUSION

FDI supports a host of benefits in the United States, notably good jobs and innovation led by research and development investment. While industrial countries are the primary source of FDI to the United States, emerging markets are becoming a bigger source of FDI and their share should be expected to increase as institutional and structural barriers in those countries decline.

Looking ahead, the United States will remain an attractive destination for foreign investment, and this investment will help bolster our economy. However, we need to continue to nurture and build upon the underlying strengths of the U.S. economy that make firms want to invest here; Including an open investment regime, a large economy, a skilled labor forced, community colleges, world-class research universities, predictable and stable regulatory regime, adequately capacitated infrastructure, and new energy sources.

End Notes

[1] These seven European countries, in descending order of direct investment in the U.S. from 2010 to 2012, are: the United Kingdom, Switzerland, Luxembourg, the Netherlands, Germany, France, and Belgium.

[2] UNCTAD World Investment Report, Annex table 01, http://unctad.org/en/Pages/DIAE/World%20Investment%20Report/Annex-Tables.aspx

The combined inflows to mainland China and Hong Kong were larger than those to the United States in 2012.

However, under the "One Country, Two Systems" principle, transactions in direct investment between Hong Kong and mainland China are treated as external transactions. Hong Kong FDI data include investments from China. Likewise, inflows to mainland China include investments from Hong Kong.

[3] Friedman, J., Gerlowski, D.A., Silberman, J., 2006. "What Attracts Foreign Multinational Corporations? Evidence from Branch Plant Location in the United States," Journal of Regional Science 32(4), 403-418.

[4] DeNavas-Walt, C., Proctor, B., Smith, J., 2013. "Income, Poverty, and Health Insurance Coverage in the United States: 2012," U.S. Census Bureau.

[5] See http://acetool.commerce.gov/regulatory-compliance-costs.

[6] Please refer to Department of Commerce's Assess Costs Everywhere website for further details. http://acetool.commerce.gov/

[7] http://www.wipo.int/pressroom/en/articles/2013/article_0016.html

[8] http://acetool.commerce.gov/intellectual-property

[9] http://www.gpo.gov/fdsys/pkg/BILLS-112hr1249enr/pdf/BILLS-112hr1249enr.pdf

[10] http://www.uspto.gov/web/offices/pac/mpep/mpep-9015-appx-l.html#al_d1b0d9_16b04_f6

[11] Maskus, K., 2000. "Intellectual Property Rights in the Global Economy", Institute for International Economics, Washington D.C., provides a comprehensive analysis of policy reform issues pertaining to IP protection; Fink, C., and Maskus, K.E, (Eds), 2005. "Intellectual Property and Development: Lessons from Recent Economic Research," World Bank, Washington, D.C., present a set of empirical studies that assess the effects of stronger standards of protection on measures of various economics and social performance.

[12] http://www.bea.gov/scb/pdf/2013/09%20September/0913_inward_direct_investment_tables.pdf, Table 2 in current costs and market value.

[13] Years in which global real GDP growth, as published in the International Monetary Fund's World Economic Outlook Database, falls below 3 percent are commonly referred to as periods of global recession, or global economic slowdowns.

[14] Because of data availability, these estimates do not include a current cost adjustment.

[15] Holding companies hold investments of other companies. The industry categorization of these other companies is not reported. An example of a non-bank holding company is a financial holding company participating in banking-related activities including insurance underwriting, securities dealing and underwriting, etc. Further information is available from https://www.ffiec.gov/nicpubweb/Content/HELP/Institution%20Type%20Description.htm.

[16] This section analyzes "majority-owned" U.S. inbound foreign direct investment for reasons of data availability. Although the vast number of affiliates are majority owned, there are important foreign investments in U.S. businesses that involve less than a 50 percent foreign ownership stake

[17] These estimates are based on the industry of sales. See box note titled "Using Employment Data to Estimate Affiliate Shares of the U.S. Economy by Industry" in "U.S. Affiliates of Foreign Companies: Operations in 2010," Survey of Current Business, August 2012.

[18] Data on all U.S. business R&D expenditures are available from the National Science Foundation, http://nsf.gov/statistics/industry/.

[19] Wholesale trade is an industry not necessarily associated with R&D. The relatively high share of R&D expenditures may stem from the fact that each U.S. affiliate is classified in a single industry, even though a single affiliate may be involved in a wide range of business activities. In particular, among U.S. affiliates, the wholesale trade industry includes many companies that also have substantial activities in manufacturing.

In: Foreign Investment in the U.S.
Editor: Theodore L. Newell
ISBN: 978-1-62948-930-8

Chapter 2

FOREIGN DIRECT INVESTMENT IN THE UNITED STATES: AN ECONOMIC ANALYSIS*

James K. Jackson

SUMMARY

Foreign direct investment in the United States rebounded slowly after falling from the $310 billion recorded in 2008, a record surpassed only by the $320 billion invested in 2000 in U.S. businesses and real estate. According to preliminary data, foreign direct investment in the United States in 2012 fell from the amount recorded in 2011. (Note: The United States defines foreign direct investment as the ownership or control, directly or indirectly, by one foreign person [individual, branch, partnership, association, government, etc.] of 10% or more of the voting securities of an incorporated U.S. business enterprise or an equivalent interest in an unincorporated U.S. business enterprise (15 CFR §806.15 [a][1]). In 2011, according to U.S. Department of Commerce data, foreigners invested $234 billion in U.S. businesses and real estate. Foreign direct investments are highly sought after by many state and local governments that are struggling to create additional jobs in their localities. While some in Congress encourage such investment to offset the perceived negative economic effects of U.S. firms investing abroad, others are

* This is an edited, reformatted and augmented version of the Congressional Research Service Publication, CRS Report for Congress RS21857, dated May 17, 2013.

concerned about foreign acquisitions of U.S. firms that are considered essential to U.S. national and economic security.

Recent Investments

Foreigners invested $234 billion in nominal terms in U.S. businesses and real estate in 2011, according to data published by the Department of Commerce.[1] According to preliminary data, foreign direct investment in the United States in 2012 was about $175 billion, a drop of 25% from the amount invested in 2011. As **Figure 1** shows, this represents a 14% increase over the $155 billion invested in 2010. Investments abroad by U.S. parent firms increased by 28% in 2011 to $419 billion, up from the $328 billion they invested abroad in 2010. The increase in foreign direct investment flows mirrors a rebound in global flows following the sharp drop in direct investment flows in 2009 and 2010. According to the United Nations' World Investment Report, global foreign direct investment inflows decreased by 38% in 2009 compared with the amount invested in 2008. Such investment rose by 13% in 2010 and by 16% in 2011 to reach $1.5 trillion, short of the $2.0 trillion invested globally in 2007.

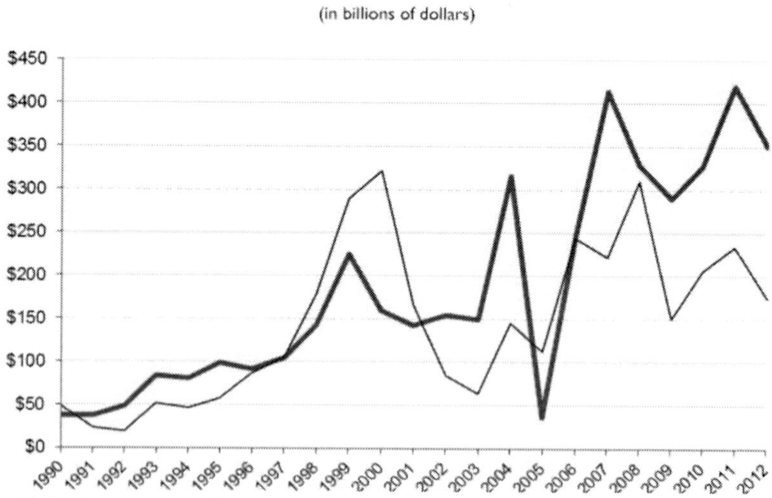

Source: U.S. Department of Commerce.

Figure 1. Foreign Direct Investment in the United States and U.S. Direct Investment Abroad, Annual Flows, 1990-2012.

According to preliminary data, U.S. direct investment abroad in 2012 was about $350 billion, a drop of 16% from the amount invested in 2011.[2] Similarly, foreign direct investment in the United States in 2012 dropped by 25% from the amount invested in 2011. U.S. direct investment abroad slowed due to reductions in reinvested earnings, intercompany debt investment, and net equity investment. Despite increases in income and earnings in 2012 compared with 2011, foreign direct investment in the United States fell by $60 billion to $175 billion in 2012, a drop of 25% compared with the $234 billion invested in 2011, due to a sharp reduction in net equity investment and in intercompany debt.

The cumulative amount, or stock, of foreign direct investment in the United States on a historical cost basis[3] rose from $2.26 trillion in 2010 to about $2.55 trillion in 2011. This marked an increase of 12.5%.[4] The Department of Commerce does not attempt to deflate the annual nominal amounts for direct investment with a specific price deflator. Instead, the department publishes alternative estimates based on current cost and market value to provide other measures of the value of direct investment.

As a share of the total amount of nonresidential investment spending in the U.S. economy, investment spending by foreign firms was equivalent to 11% in 2011, far below the 20% reached in 2009. Better credit conditions and a slight rise in the rate of growth in the U.S. economy tended to push up such mainstays of foreign direct investment activity as mergers and acquisitions. The rise in the value of foreign direct investment includes increases in equity capital, reinvested earnings, and a smaller increase in intercompany debt. Equity values, which accounted for 40% of the total amount of foreign direct investment in 2011, fell by nearly one-third from that recorded in 2010. Reinvested earnings rose by nearly 30% to account for 37% of total foreign direct investment, as U.S. affiliates relied more on their own earnings than on funds borrowed from their foreign parent companies. Intercompany debt accounted for the rest of the total amount of foreign direct investment, or about 23%. In comparison, U.S. direct investment abroad in 2011 was comprised almost entirely of reinvested earnings.

Foreign direct investments in the U.S. manufacturing sector as a whole in 2011 were higher than in 2010 and accounted for nearly half of the overall increase in foreign direct investment in 2011. Foreign direct investment in the banking, finance, retail trade, and professional services all increased in 2011, compared with investments in 2010. In comparison, investments were down in the wholesale trade, real estate, and information sectors. Data for the first two quarters of 2012 indicate that foreign direct investment in the United States is down about 41% from the amount recorded in the comparable period in 2011. Such investments may well continue to lag behind similar investment in 2010 in the second half of the year if the rate of economic growth stalls.

With over $441 billion invested in the United States, the United Kingdom is the largest foreign direct investor, as is indicated in **Table 1**. Japan is the second-largest foreign direct investor in the U.S. economy with about $289 billion in investments. Following the Japanese are the Dutch ($240 billion), the Germans ($215 billion), the Swiss ($212 billion), the Canadians ($211 billion), the French ($199 billion) and Luxembourg ($190).

In some cases, investments by one or two countries dominate certain industrial sectors, suggesting that there is a rough form of international specialization present in the investment patterns of foreign multinational firms. At year end 2011, the cumulative amount of investment, or the investment position measured at historical cost, indicates that the Netherlands and the United Kingdom accounted for the bulk of foreign investments in the U.S. petroleum sector, reflecting investments by two giant companies: Royal Dutch Shell and British Petroleum. Japanese investments in the U.S. wholesale trade sector are also substantial, followed by British investments, and European investors account for the bulk of foreign investments in the retail trade sector. German investors are the largest investors in the information sector as a result of a number of large media company acquisitions. French, German, and British investments dominate other foreign investments in the banking sector, while Dutch, Canadian, British, and French investments account for over half of the investments in the finance sector. Britain's $87 billion investment in the U.S. finance and insurance sectors surpasses the more than approximately $74 billion invested in the finance sector alone by British firms (data for banking have been suppressed by the Department of Commerce), followed by Japan ($35 billion) and Canada ($34 billion), although investments in the U.S. banking sector by Germany and France likely are larger than investments by either Japan or Canada. Foreign direct investment in the U.S. manufacturing sector is dominated by a number of countries, each with substantial investments: investments by the United Kingdom ($140 billion), Switzerland ($106 billion), the Netherlands ($101 billion), Japan ($83 billion), Luxembourg ($69 billion), Germany ($64 billion), and France ($60 billion) account for nearly three-fourths of the total amount of foreign direct investment in this sector.

Investment spending by developed economies accounts for 95% of all foreign direct investment in the United States. These investments are predominately in the manufacturing sector, which accounts for about 33% of foreign direct investment in the United States, a decline from periods when such investment accounted for a majority share of the total. Another 21% of foreign direct investment is in the banking and finance sectors, and 14% is in the retail and wholesale trade sectors, reflecting purchases of department stores and other investments to assist foreign firms in marketing and distributing their products. The fast-growing information sector accounts for 5.8%, while real estate and services account for modest shares of 1.9% and 3.5%, respectively. All other industries account for the remaining 21%.

ACQUISITIONS AND ESTABLISHMENTS

Another way of looking at foreign direct investment is by distinguishing between transactions in which foreigners acquire existing U.S. firms and those in which foreigners establish new firms— termed "greenfield" investments. New investments are often preferred at the local level because they are thought to add to local employment, whereas a foreign acquisition itself may add little, if any, new employment. In 2008, outlays for new investments, which include investments made directly by foreign investors and those made by existing U.S. affiliates, were $260 billion, a 3.0% increase over the $252 billion invested in 2007. According to the Department of Commerce, the increase in new investments reflected several large transactions.[5] These transactions include the acquisition of Anheuser-Busch Cos. Inc., by Stichting Interbrew SA for $52 billion; the acquisition of Alcon Inc., by Novartis AG for $10.8 billion; and large investments in Commerce Bancorp, New Jersey, Morgan Stanley, and Citigroup. Acquisitions of existing U.S. firms accounted for 93% of the new investments by value. Investments by the existing U.S. affiliates of foreign firms accounted for 82% of the total transactions by investor, while other foreign direct investors accounted for the remaining 18% of transactions. Investment outlays by foreign firms increased from 2007 to 2008 in all major sectors, except wholesale trade, retail trade, and real estate. Investment in information, manufacturing, and services all posted increases. The Department of Commerce halted publication of the annual report on foreign acquisitions after the June 2008 edition. Instead, it is developing a separate report that it expects will better capture the construction of new plants by foreign-owned firms that are operating in the United States.

Table 1. Foreign Direct Investment Position in the United States on a Historical-Cost Basis at Year-End 2011 (in billions of U.S. dollars)

All	All industries	Manufacturing	Wholesale trade	Retail trade	Information	Banking	Finance	Real estate	Services	Other industries
All countries	**$2,547.8**	**$838.3**	**$310.0**	**$50.6**	**$147.1**	**$153.1**	**$376.8**	**$48.4**	**$88.1**	**535.6**
Canada	210.9	32.3	6.8	(D)	0.8	34.3	62.9	2.2	(D)	64.9
Europe	**1,811.9**	**676.1**	**163.1**	**38.9**	**134.3**	**71.1**	**298.2**	**23.3**	**56.1**	**350.8**
Austria	4.8	2.3	0.4	(D)	0.0	(D)	0.0	0.0	(D)	0.1
Belgium	86.0	50.3	19.6	7.1	(D)	(D)	(D)	0.0	0.0	6.2
France	198.7	60.2	31.3	(D)	13.8	9.3	(D)	0.5	6.8	39.6
Germany	215.9	64.0	24.0	3.7	48.9	11.4	42.7	8.2	0.1	12.8
Ireland	25.0	11.8	0.9	0.0	(D)	0.2	4.2	0.0	(D)	2.3
Italy	23.0	7.5	1.4	3.0	(D)	(D)	(D)	0.1	(D)	(D)
Luxembourg	190.4	69.2	5.3	(D)	16.8	0.0	45.9	1.8	(D)	49.4
Netherlands	240.3	100.9	27.4	2.4	8.2	(D)	37.4	3.1	32.1	(D)
Sweden	42.3	29.6	6.6	(D)	0.5	(D)	0.1	0.9	(D)	1.4
Switzerland	211.7	106.0	9.4	6.3	(D)	(D)	44.8	0.6	0.4	44.7
UK	442.2	139.9	25.8	3.5	26.3	(D)	87.2	4.9	(D)	(D)
L. America	**85.7**	**(D)**	**7.3**	**(D)**	**0.9**	**4.2**	**-14.1**	**12.2**	**(D)**	**48.2**

All	**All industries**	**Manufacturing**	**Wholesale trade**	**Retail trade**	**Information**	**Banking**	**Finance**	**Real estate**	**Services**	**Other industries**
Africa	**4.3**	**(D)**	**0.6**	**(D)**	**0.0**	**(D)**	**(D)**	**(D)**	**(D)**	**(D)**
Mid. East	**25.4**	**(D)**	**6.9**	**(D)**	**0.8**	**(D)**	**(D)**	**(D)**	**(D)**	**(D)**
Asia	**409.7**	**111.9**	**125.3**	**5.1**	**10.2**	**42.0**	**29.5**	**8.9**	**11.8**	**65.1**
Australia	55.9	5.2	0.2	(D)	(D)	2.9	4.1	2.0	0.4	40.7
Japan	289.5	82.7	103.2	4.8	9.9	35.0	22.1	6.3	8.6	16.9
Korea	18.4	3.1	14.0	0.0	0.0	0.1	0.2	(D)	0.0	(D)
OPEC	14.4	(D)	(D)	D)	0.0	0.9	(D)	(D)	0.0	2.9

Source: Lowe, Jeffrey H., Direct Investment Positions for 2009-2011: Detailed Historical-Cost Positions and Related Financial and Income Flows, Survey of Current Business, September 2012. p. 80.

Notes: The position is the stock, or cumulative, book value of foreign direct investors' equity in, and net outstanding loans to, their U.S. affiliates. A negative position may result as U.S. affiliates repay debts to their foreign parents, and as foreign parents borrow funds from their U.S. affiliates. "D" indicates that data have been suppressed by the Department of Commerce to avoid the disclosure of data of individual companies.

ECONOMIC PERFORMANCE

By year-end 2010, the latest year for which detailed data are available, foreign firms employed almost 6 million Americans, less than 4% of the U.S. civilian labor force, and owned over 33,000 individual business establishments.[6] Foreign firms have a direct investment presence in every state. Employment of these firms ranges from over 636,000 in California, to about 7,700 in South Dakota. Following California, New York (459,600), Texas (455,200), Pennsylvania (285,300), Illinois (263,800), New Jersey (256,700), and Florida (239,500) have the largest numbers of residents employed by foreign firms. In 2010, 36% of the foreign firms' employment was in the manufacturing sector, more than twice the share of manufacturing employment in the U.S. economy as a whole, with average annual compensation (wages and benefits) per worker of about $76,000.

Retail and wholesale trade accounted for another 21% of total affiliate employment. Dutch-affiliated firms are the largest single employers in the retail trade sector and account for nearly one-third of total affiliate employment in this sector, while Japanese and German firms account for over half of the employment in the wholesale trade sector. Canadian, French, and Japanese firms account for the largest share of affiliate employment in the services sector, which accounted for about 20% of total affiliate employment. Employment in the information, finance, and real estate services sectors accounts for another 14% of total affiliate employment. Average employee compensation is highest in the finance sector—$159,000—where British, Canadian, Swiss, French, and Dutch firms account for three-fourths of the employment. The rest of the affiliate employment is spread among a large number of other industries.

The affiliates of foreign firms spent $163 billion in the United States in 2010 on new plants and equipment, imported $542 billion in goods, and exported $250 billion in goods. Since 1980, the total amount of foreign direct investment in the economy has increased eight-fold and nearly doubled as a share of U.S. gross domestic product (GDP) from 3.4% to 6.4%. It is important to note, however, that these data do not imply anything in particular about the role foreign direct investment has played in the rate of growth of U.S. GDP.

The performance of foreign-owned establishments, on average, compared with their U.S.-owned counterparts presents a mixed picture. Historically, foreign-owned firms operating in the United States have had lower rates of return, as measured by return on assets, than U.S.-owned firms, although the gap between the two groups appears to have narrowed over time. According to the Bureau of Economic Analysis, this narrowing of the gap in the rate of return appears to be related to age effects, or the costs associated with acquiring or establishing a new business that can entail startup costs that disappear over time and market share.[7] By other measures, foreign-owned manufacturing firms appear to be outperforming their U.S. counterparts.[8] Although foreign-owned firms account for less than 3% of all U.S. manufacturing establishments, they have had six times more value added on average and seven times higher value of shipments than other manufacturing establishments. The average plant size for foreign-owned firms is much larger— six times—than for other U.S. firms, on average, in similar industries. This difference in plant size apparently rises from an absence of small plants among those that are foreign-owned. As a result of the larger plant scale and newer plant age, foreign-owned firms paid wages on average that were 60% higher than other U.S. manufacturing firms, had 40% higher productivity per worker, and had 58% greater output per worker than the average of comparable U.S.-owned manufacturing plants. Foreign-owned firms also display higher capital intensity in a larger number of industries than all U.S. establishments.

These differences between foreign-owned firms and all U.S. firms should be viewed with some caution. First, the two groups of firms are not strictly comparable: the group of foreign-owned firms comprises a subset of all foreign firms, which includes primarily very large firms; the group of U.S. firms includes all firms, spanning a broader range of sizes. Secondly, the differences reflect a range of additional factors, including the prospect that foreign firms that invest in the United States likely are large firms with proven technologies or techniques they have successfully transferred to the United States. Small foreign ventures, experimenting with unproven technologies, are unlikely to want the added risk of investing overseas. Foreign investors also tend to opt for larger scale and higher capital-intensity plants than the average U.S. firm to offset the risks inherent in investing abroad and to generate higher profits to make it economical to manage an operation far removed from the parent firm.

Conclusion

Foreign direct investment in the United States in 2010 rose sharply over the amount invested in 2009, but did not rise to the record levels of such investment recorded in previous years. Other countries have experienced a similar turnaround in foreign direct investment inflows, especially some of the less developed economies where there is a great potential for investment. As the rate of growth of the U.S. economy improves relative to other advanced economies, interest rates stay low, and the rate of price inflation stays in check, foreign direct investment in the United States likely will continue to increase. Of particular importance will be public concerns over foreign direct investment in the economy as a whole and on the overall phenomenon referred to as "globalization," with its impact on jobs in the economy. Concerns over foreign direct investment, where they exist, stem not so much from the perceived potential losses of international competitiveness that characterized similar concerns in the 1980s, but from potential job losses that could result from mergers and acquisitions, although such losses could occur whether the acquiring company is foreign- or U.S.-owned. Such concerns are offset, at least in part, by the benefits that are perceived to be derived from the inflow of capital and the potential for new jobs being created in local areas.

Although job security is an important public issue, opposition to some types of foreign direct investment stems from concerns about the impact of such investment on U.S. economic and security interests, particularly in light of the terrorist attacks of September 11, 2001. The U.S. economy, however, remains a prime destination for foreign direct investment. As the pace of economic growth in the nation increases relative to that of foreign economies, foreign direct investment likely will increase as new investments are attracted to the United States and existing firms are encouraged to reinvest profits in their U.S. operations.

End Notes

[1] Scott, Sarah P., U.S. International Transactions: First Quarter of 2012. *Survey of Current Business*, July 2012, p. 59. Direct investment data reported in the balance of payments differ from capital flow data reported elsewhere, because the balance of payments data have not been adjusted for current cost adjustments to earnings.

[2] Scott, Sarah P., U.S. International Transactions: Fourth Quarter and Year 2012. *Survey of Current Business*, April 2013, p. 28.

[3] The position, or stock, is the net book value of foreign direct investors' equity in, and outstanding loans to, their affiliates in the United States. A change in the position in a given year consists of three components: equity and intercompany inflows, reinvested earnings of incorporated affiliates, and valuation adjustments to account for changes in the value of financial assets. The Department of Commerce also publishes data on the foreign direct investment position valued on a current-cost and market value bases. These estimates indicate that in 2011 foreign direct investment increased by $311 billion measured at

current cost to a cumulative value of \$2.9 trillion, while the market value measure rose by \$112 billion in to reach a cumulative value of \$3.5 trillion.

[4] Barefoot, Kevin B., and Marilyn Ibarra-Caton, Direct Investment Positions for 2011: Country and Industry Detail, *Survey of Current Business*, July 2012. p. 20.

[5] Anderson, Thomas, Foreign Direct Investment in the United States: New Investment in 2008. *Survey of Current Business*, June 2009. p. 34.

[6] *Foreign Direct Investment in the United States: Operations of U.S. Affiliates of Foreign Companies, Preliminary2010 Estimates*. Bureau of Economic Analysis, September 2012, Table 1A-1.

[7] Mataloni, Raymond J. Jr., An Examination of the Low Rates of Return of Foreign-Owned U.S. Companies, *Survey of Current Business*, March 2000, p. 55.

[8] *Foreign Direct Investment in the United States, Establishment Data for 2002*, Bureau of Economic Analysis, June2007.

In: Foreign Investment in the U.S.
Editor: Theodore L. Newell
ISBN: 978-1-62948-930-8

Chapter 3

FOREIGN INVESTMENT IN THE UNITED STATES: MAJOR FEDERAL STATUTORY RESTRICTIONS*

Michael V. Seitzinger

SUMMARY

Foreign investment in the United States is a matter of congressional concern. It is believed by some that the United States has an unusually liberal policy which allows foreigners to invest in virtually all American businesses and real estate and that these foreign investments undermine the American economy by making it vulnerable to foreign influence and domination. These critics argue that there is even foreign domination of some key defense-related industries and that the ability of the country to protect itself in a time of national emergency could greatly suffer. These critics further argue that extensive foreign investment in this country drives up prices which Americans have to pay for investments and, even more importantly, for houses and farmland in areas where there is a significant amount of foreign ownership.

However, others argue that the United States should welcome foreign investment because the influx of foreign money contributes to the creation of jobs in this country. Some also believe that the United States should be a kind

* This is an edited, reformatted and augmented version of the Congressional Research Service Publication, CRS Report for Congress RL33103, dated June 17, 2013.

of sanctuary for foreign money because of the political and economic instability which characterizes much of the rest of the world. It is also argued that, in this age of globalization of the world's economy, United States restrictions on foreign investment will only impair this nation's economy and cause us to appear isolationist.

This report takes a look at some of the major federal statutes which presently restrict investment by foreigners. The report first gives a brief history of foreign investment in the United States. It then reviews constitutional justifications and constitutional limitations which exist concerning federal statutory restrictions on foreign ownership of property. After that follows a discussion of some of the major federal statutes which limit foreign investment in the United States. Some of these statutes will be looked at in detail, but a detailed treatment of such other laws as the tax laws, the antitrust laws, and the immigration laws is beyond the scope of this report.

HISTORY OF FOREIGN INVESTMENT IN THE UNITED STATES

Traditionally accepted principles of international law state that the sovereign powers of a nation include the power to exclude alien persons and property.[1] However, in most cases, so as to be mutually beneficial to commerce, nations usually do not fully exercise this power of exclusion. Sometimes a nation writes the restraints into its domestic law. For example, Clause XXX of the Magna Carta has the following provision:

> All merchants, if they were not openly prohibited before, shall have their safe and sure Conduct to depart out of England, to come into England, to tarry in, and go through England, as well by land as by water, to buy and sell without any manner of (evil tolts)[2] by the old and rightful Customers, except in time of war; and if they be of a Land making War against Us, and be found in our Realm at the beginning of the wars, they shall be attached without harm of body or goods, until it be known unto Us, or our Chief Justice, how our Merchants be entered therein the Land making War against Us; and if our merchants be well entreated there, theirs shall be likewise with Us.

Treaties and other forms of bilateral and multicultural agreements have also restricted foreign persons and property. For example, the Greek city-states formed agreements which allowed the reciprocal entry of and ownership of property of foreigners from other contracting states.[3]

The United States has through the years accepted both kinds of restraint.[4] The American colonies were formed to realize profits for their English and Continental investors. After the War of Independence, the new government moved quickly to resolve the outstanding foreign claims so as to assure creditworthiness and to provide a favorable climate for foreign investment. The Jay Treaty, for example, stated that the new United States government would compensate the British for any property which had been seized or destroyed and for unpaid debts caused by the Revolution.

In his Report on Manufactures in 1791, Alexander Hamilton urged the new nation to keep investment open to foreigners.

> It is not impossible that there may be persons disposed to look with a jealous eye on the introduction of foreign capital, as if it were an instrument to deprive our own citizens of the profits of our own industry; but, perhaps, there never could be a more unreasonable jealousy. Instead of being viewed as a rival, it ought to be considered as a most valuable auxiliary, conducing to put in motion a greater quantity of productive labor, and a greater portion of useful enterprise, than could exist without it.[5]

Hamilton's ideas prevailed. During the 18th and 19th centuries, foreign capital contributed enormously to the nation's development.

> As the nation grew, its roads, bridges, canals, banks, and finally railroads were largely financed by state bonds sold overseas. The Erie Canal, the first American canal to achieve commercial success, was made possible by the first state bonds to be quoted on the London market, in 1817. Europe was eager for investments such as these, and a group of Anglo- American banking houses were established in London—led by Baring Brothers—which specialized in American finance. They bought up entire issues for resale in England. In their eagerness for foreign capital, American states and private enterprises sent their agents to Europe. Generals and congressmen turned to bond selling….[6]

By the middle of the 19th century, foreigners held half of the federal and state and one-quarter of the municipal debts. The 1849 California Gold Rush sparked even more foreign investment.

It is also interesting to note that American real estate was quite popular with foreign investors. Europeans acquired substantial holdings in such states as New York, Maine, Florida, West Virginia, and Iowa. The state of Texas granted an English company 3 million acres in payment for building the state capitol building in Austin. Some of the titled Europeans, including the German Baron von Richthofen and the British Earl of Dunraven, attempted to create baronial estates in the West.

At the turn of the century, with the invention of the automobile and the increasing importance of oil, foreign oil companies, such as Royal Dutch Shell, began buying American properties. However, World War I made a drastic change in the influx of foreign capital into the United States. The creditor countries of Europe sold many of their American holdings in order to supply their wartime needs. In just a few years, the United States shifted from a debtor to a creditor nation, a position which it retained for a number of years.[7]

Throughout the nation's history, there has been criticism of foreign investment in the United States. When the first and second banks of the United States were created in 1791 and 1816, their organic statutes barred the election of aliens as directors. The Know-Nothing Party advocated discriminatory taxation of foreign capital as early as the 1850s. The Alien Land Law of 1887 prohibited aliens from owning land in federal territories.[8] During the 20th century Congress passed a number of statutes aimed at restricting foreign investment in certain industries such as shipping, aviation, and communications. Nevertheless, by the early 1970s foreign investment in the United States began to rise dramatically, and since then there has been frequent congressional debate as to whether there should be more restriction on investment by foreign citizens in American businesses.

CONSTITUTIONAL JUSTIFICATIONS AND LIMITATIONS

Federal constitutional provisions may be interpreted as legal validation of federal statutes restricting investments by foreigners; other constitutional provisions have to be adhered to by the states in imposing additional restrictions on foreign investment.

The federal government is a government of limited powers. There is no express constitutional provision permitting the regulation of foreign investment in the United States. Thus, other federal powers mentioned in the Constitution must be looked at to justify such regulation. Three constitutional bases for such legislation are the federal powers over immigration and naturalization,[9] the federal power to regulate interstate and foreign commerce,[10] and the power to provide for the national defense.[11]

Congress has the exclusive power to establish naturalization and citizenship requirements and to admit and expel aliens.

> That the government of the United States, through the action of the legislative department, can exclude aliens from its territory is a proposition which we do not think open to controversy. Jurisdiction over its own territory to that extent is an incident of every independent nation. It is a part of its independence. If it could not exclude aliens, it would be to that extent subject to the control of another power.... The United States, in their relation to foreign countries and their subjects or citizens, are one nation, invested with powers which belong to independent nations, the exercise of which can be invoked for the maintenance of its absolute independence and security throughout its entire territory.[12]

Congress has also been held to have the power to regulate the conduct of alien residents and to prescribe the conditions for their admission and residency.[13] Thus, it is arguable that Congress can condition entry and residency of an alien upon his or her not acquiring investments in the United States. Although this might be an extreme condition to apply, no federal case appears to suggest limits to Congress's ability to place substantive conditions upon entry and residency of aliens.

Congress also has the exclusive power to "regulate Commerce with foreign Nations, and among the several States."[14] The Commerce Clause would appear to give Congress the power to restrict the use of instrumentalities of interstate commerce to transact the sale or exchange of property to a foreign citizen or to the representative of a foreign citizen.[15]

Finally, Congress's power to "raise and support Armies" would also appear to be a constitutional basis for restricting foreign investment in the United States. If it is determined that foreign investments impair national preparedness in the event of an emergency, it appears that prohibition of foreign investments could on this basis be construed as constitutional.

Further, it should be noted that the federal government has exclusive authority over foreign relations. In the case *Zschernig* v. *Miller*,[16] the Supreme Court held unconstitutional an Oregon statute which provided for the escheat to the state of property which would otherwise pass to a nonresident alien unless the laws of the foreign nation had reciprocal rights for United States citizens. The Oregon statute required the local probate courts to inquire into:

> aliens under their law have enforceable rights, whether the so-called "rights" are merely dispensations turning upon the whim or caprice of government officials, whether the representation of consuls, ambassadors, and other representatives of foreign nations is credible or made in good faith, whether there is the actual administration in the particular foreign system of law any element of confiscation.[17]

The Court found the Oregon statute to be unconstitutional because it infringed upon the exclusively federal authority over foreign relations.

On the other hand, it has been stated that:

> The imposition of any significant investment controls would likely violate both the spirit and the letter of more than forty bilateral treaties regulating trade and investment relations, many of which laws have been signed within the last ten years, as well as derogating our commitment to the OECD Code of Liberalization of Capital Movements.[18]

The treaties mentioned in the above quotation are Treaties of Friendship, Commerce, and Navigation which grant foreign countries the right to enter, trade, invest, or establish and operate businesses in the other signatory country. Thus, any foreign investment statute would need to take into account those Friendship, Commerce, and Navigation Treaties to which the United States is a signatory.

Further, treaties such as the North American Free Trade Agreement (NAFTA) among the United States, Canada, and Mexico provide for foreign investment opportunities. Chapter 11 of NAFTA requires each party to "accord to investors of another Party treatment no less favorable than it accords, in like circumstances, to its own investors with respect to the establishment, acquisition, expansion, management, conduct, operation, and sale or other disposition of investments."

Other constitutional provisions may be interpreted to protect foreigners from certain acts of state and local governments. Because the Due Process and Equal Protection Clauses of the Fourteenth Amendment to the United States Constitution apply to *persons* instead of to *citizens*, these provisions guarantee that states cannot abridge the rights of foreign nationals within the United States.[19] The Supreme Court has in the past voided state laws which establish classifications in government actions solely on the basis of citizenship. In doing so, the Court has stated that a classification based solely upon citizenship or nationality is inherently suspect and subject to strict scrutiny. For example, in *Graham* v. *Richardson*[20] the Court held that state laws which denied welfare benefits to resident aliens who had not resided in the United States for a required number of years were unconstitutional because they deprived these persons of equal protection of the laws.

> Under traditional equal protection principles, a State retains broad discretion to classify as long as its classification has a reasonable basis [citations omitted]. This is so in "the area of economics and social welfare" [citations omitted]. But the Court's decisions have established that classifications based on alienage, like those based on nationality or race, are inherently suspect and subject to close judicial scrutiny. Aliens as a class are a prime example of a "discrete and insular" minority [citations omitted] for whom such heightened judicial solicitude is appropriate. Accordingly, it was said in *Takahashi*, 334 U.S. at 420, that "the power of a state to apply its laws exclusively to its alien inhabitants as a class is confined within narrow limits."[21]

As mentioned in the *Takahashi* case[22] in the above quotation, a state must be careful in applying state laws exclusively to aliens. This case challenged a California statute which barred the issuance of commercial fishing licenses to persons ineligible for citizenship. The Supreme Court held that this statute violated the Fourteenth Amendment's Equal Protection Clause and the federal laws concerning citizenship.

Citizenship has also been rejected as a legitimate classification concerning membership in a state bar,[23] complete bans on employment of aliens in the state civil service system,[24] and the granting of educational benefits to aliens.[25] Yet, the Supreme Court has limited the application of these protections in other cases, one concerning a New York statute limiting appointment to the state police force to United States citizens,[26] and another concerning a New York statute forbidding certification of a non-citizen as a public school teacher unless the person had evidenced intent to become a citizen.[27] Therefore, there appears to be an exception to the general rule that a classification based on citizenship is subject to strict judicial scrutiny in situations where the classification relates to an essential governmental, political, or constitutional function. In such situations the less strict, rational basis test may be applied. From this discussion it may be concluded that state laws restricting investments by at least resident aliens may come under strict judicial scrutiny.[28]

Yet, it must be remembered that, in contrast to the states, the federal government has broad authority over naturalization and immigration.

> For reasons long recognized as valid, the responsibility for regulating the relationship between the United States and our alien visitors has been committed to the political branches of the Federal Government. Since decisions in these matters may implicate our relations with foreign powers, and since a wide variety of classifications must be defined in the light of changing political and economic circumstances, such decisions are frequently of a character appropriate to either the Legislature or the Executive than to the Judiciary.[29]

The Supreme Court has held, for example, that aliens can be denied Medicare coverage[30] and that the federal government can deny a visa to a Marxist invited to speak on world communism.[31] The power of Congress to exclude aliens from the United States and to prescribe the terms and conditions on which they enter is virtually absolute and is an attribute of the sovereignty of the United States.[32]

PRESENT FEDERAL RESTRICTIONS ON FOREIGN INVESTMENT

Four major federal statutes which have an impact upon foreign investment in the United States are information-gathering and disclosure statutes, instead of actual restriction statutes. One of these statutes is the International Investment and Trade in Services Survey Act of 1976.[33] Congress intended this act:

> to provide clear and unambiguous authority for the President to collect information on international investment and United States foreign trade in services, whether directly or by affiliates, including related information necessary for assessing the impact of such investment and trade, to authorize the collection and use of information on direct investments owned or controlled directly or indirectly by foreign governments or persons, and to provide analyses of such information to the Congress, the executive agencies, and the general public.[34]

The President by executive order delegated responsibility under this act for studying direct investment to the Commerce Department and portfolio investment to the Treasury Department.[35] The act directs the President to conduct a benchmark survey of foreign direct investment in the United States every five years.[36] Amendments to the act in 1990 direct the President to publish for the use of the general public and federal agencies periodic information concerning foreign investment, including information on ownership by foreign governments of United States affiliates of business enterprises the ownership or control of which by foreign persons is more than 50% of the voting securities or other evidence of ownership of these enterprises, as well as business enterprises the ownership or control of which by foreign persons is 50% or less of the voting securities or other evidence of ownership of these enterprises.[37] The 1990 Amendments also provide that the President may request a report from the Bureau of Economic Analysis (BEA) of the Department of Commerce of the best available information on the extent of foreign direct investment in a given industry.[38]

Another federal statute having an impact upon foreign investment in the United States is the Foreign Direct Investment and International Financial Data Improvements Act of 1990.[39] The purpose of this act is:

> to allow the Department of Commerce's Bureau of Economic Analysis (BEA) access to information collected by the Bureau of the Census (Census). This access will improve the accuracy and analysis of BEA's reports to the public and to Congress on foreign direct investment in the United States.[40]

This act, among other requirements, adds chapter 10 to title 13 of the United States Code to provide that the Bureau of the Census shall exchange with the Bureau of Economic Analysis of the Department of Commerce any information that is collected under the census provisions and under the International Investment and Trade in Services Survey Act that pertains to a business enterprise operating in the United States if the Secretary of Commerce determines that the information is appropriate to augment and improve the quality of the data collected under the Survey Act. The Data Improvements Act of 1990 also requires that other reports be prepared by the Secretary of Commerce and the Comptroller General and submitted to congressional committees.[41] The Bureau of the Census may provide business data to the Bureau of Economic Analysis and the Bureau of Labor Statistics (BLS) if the information is required for an authorized statistical purpose and the provision is the subject of a written agreement with that Designated Statistical Agency or its successors.[42]

The third of these information-gathering and disclosure statutes is the Agricultural Foreign Investment Disclosure Act of 1978.[43] This act has the following two major requirements: (1) any foreign person who acquires or transfers any interest, other than a security interest, in agricultural land must submit a report to the Secretary of Agriculture not later than 90 days after the date of the acquisition or transfer;[44] (2) any foreign person who holds any interest, other than a security interest, in agricultural land on the day before the effective date of this act must submit a report to the Secretary of Agriculture not later than 180 days after the effective date of the act.[45]

The fourth statute is also a disclosure statute. It is known as the Domestic and Foreign Investment Improved Disclosure Act of 1977 and is a requirement added to the Foreign Corrupt Practices Act of 1977.[46] This provision amended Section 13(d) of the Securities Exchange Act of 1934[47] to require that anyone who acquires 5% or more of the equity securities of a company registered with the Securities and Exchange Commission must disclose certain specified information, including citizenship and residence. Hearings indicate that this statute is directed at foreign investors in order to improve the ability of the federal government to monitor foreign investment in the United States.[48]

All of the statutes discussed above are information-gathering and disclosure in nature. There are not across-the-board, blanket restrictions on foreign investment in the United States. Instead, over the years Congress has believed that certain industries which could affect national security should have limits on foreign investment. These industries include the maritime industry, the aircraft industry, banking, resources and power, and the various businesses which are parties to government contracts.

Shipping Industry

Laws that have provisions concerning barriers to foreign investment in the maritime industry are dispersed throughout Title 46 of the United States Code.

In the area of merchant shipping, there are restrictions on foreign ownership of ships which are eligible for documentation in the United States. Any vessel of at least five tons that is not registered under the laws of a foreign country is eligible for documentation if it is owned by: (1) a United States citizen; (2) an association, trust, joint venture, or other entity, all of whose members are United States citizens and that is capable of holding title to a vessel under the laws of the United States or of a state; (3) a partnership whose general partners are United States citizens and whose controlling interest is owned by United States citizens; (4) a corporation established under federal or state laws whose chief executive officer and chairman of its board of directors are United States citizens and no more of its directors are noncitizens than a minority of the number necessary to constitute a quorum; (5) the United States government; or (6) a state government.[49]

Aircraft Industry

Statutory restrictions bar a considerable amount of foreign investment in the aircraft industry.

It is unlawful for any person to operate any aircraft unless it is registered.[50] An aircraft is eligible for registration only if it is: (1) not registered under the laws of a foreign country and is owned by a citizen of the United States, a citizen of a foreign country lawfully admitted for permanent residence in the United States, or a corporation not a citizen of the United States when the corporation is organized and doing business under the laws of the United States or a state and the aircraft is based and primarily used in the United States; or (2) an aircraft of the United States Government or a state, the District of Columbia, a territory or possession, or a political subdivision of a state, territory, or possession.[51] A citizen of the United States is defined as: (a) an individual who is a citizen of the United States, (b) a partnership of which each member is a United States citizen, or (c) a corporation or association organized under the laws of the United States or of any state, the District of Columbia, territory, or possession of the United States, of which the president and two-thirds or more of the board of directors and other managing officers are United States citizens, which is under the actual control of United States citizens and in which at least 75% of the voting interest is owned or controlled by persons who are citizens of the United States.[52]

Foreign aircraft which are not a part of the armed forces of a foreign nation may be navigated in the United States by airmen holding certificates or licenses issued or rendered valid by the United States or by the nation in which the aircraft is registered if the foreign nation grants a similar privilege concerning United States aircraft.[53]

Aircraft operators may be subject to restrictions based on citizenship. It is unlawful for a person to operate an aircraft without an airman certificate.[54] The Administrator of the Federal Aviation Administration may restrict or prohibit issuing an airman certificate to an alien or make issuing the certificate to an alien dependent upon a reciprocal agreement with the government of a foreign country.[55]

The Secretary of Transportation is authorized to provide insurance and reinsurance against loss or damage arising from the risk of operation of aircraft.[56] Citizenship requirements may be important in obtaining this insurance. For example, some air cargoes may be insured only if they are owned by citizens or residents of the United States.[57]

Mining

All valuable mineral deposits in lands belonging to the United States that are open to exploration and purchase may be purchased by United States citizens and by those who have declared their intention to become United States citizens.[58] Proof of citizenship may consist, in the case of an individual, of his affidavit; in the case of an association of unincorporated persons, of the affidavit of their authorized agent or upon information and belief; and in the case of a corporation organized under the laws of the United States, a state, or territory, by the filing of a certified copy of their charter or certificate of incorporation.[59]

Deposits of coal, phosphate, sodium, potassium, oil, oil shale, gilsonite, or gas and lands containing these deposits owned by the United States, including within national forests and in incorporated cities, towns, villages, and national parks and monuments, shall be subject to disposition in the approved manner to United States citizens, associations of United States citizens, or any corporation organized under United States, state, or territorial laws. Citizens of another country whose laws, customs, or regulations deny similar privileges to citizens or corporations of the United States shall not by stock ownership, stock holding, or stock control own any interest in any lease concerning these mineral lands.[60]

The leasing of oil, natural gas, and other mineral deposits is allowed in the submerged lands of the Continental Shelf.[61] Regulations require that only United States citizens, resident aliens, domestic corporations, or associations of one or more of these groups may obtain these leases.[62]

Energy

Licenses for the construction, operation, or maintenance of facilities for the development, transmission, and utilization of power on land and water over which the federal government has control may be issued only to United States citizens and domestic corporations.[63]

A license for nuclear facilities cannot be acquired by a foreign citizen or by a corporation believed to be controlled by a foreign citizen or government.[64]

Lands

There appear to be few federal restrictions on the ownership of land by foreign individuals or by foreign corporations. However, such past acts as the Homestead Act[65] required American citizenship in order to make claims on these lands. Today, the Desert Land Act requires citizenship or a declared intention of citizenship in order to make claims.[66] Also, the Secretary of the Interior continues to require American citizenship or a declared intention of citizenship for authorizing permits for grazing on public lands,[67] and, as discussed above, the Agricultural Foreign Investment Disclosure Act requires the disclosure to the Secretary of Agriculture by foreigners of agricultural land purchases in the United States. Further, public lands improved at the expense of funds from a reclamation project can be sold only to United States citizens.[68]

Communications

Federal statutes restrict foreign ownership and operation of mass communications media in the United States. Radio station licenses shall not be granted to or held by any foreign government or representative of a foreign government.[69] No broadcast or common carrier or aeronautical en route or aeronautical fixed radio station license shall be granted to or held by any alien or the representative of any alien, any corporation organized under the laws of a foreign government, any corporation of which more than one-fifth of the capital stock is owned or voted by aliens or their representatives or by a foreign government or representative or by any corporation organized under the laws of a foreign country, or by any corporation directly or indirectly controlled by any other corporation of which any officer or more than one-fourth of the capital stock is owned or voted by aliens, their representatives, or by a foreign government or representative, or by any corporation organized under the laws of a foreign country if the public interest will be served by the refusal or revocation of the license.[70]

There does not appear to be a federal statute prohibiting the investment by foreign citizens in United States newspapers and magazines. However, the Foreign Agents Registration Act[71] requires that agents of foreign principals must register with the Attorney General of the United States, that informational materials for or in the interests of a foreign principal must be labeled to show the relationship between the agent and the foreign principal, and that the agent must file two copies of the printed propaganda with the Justice Department.[72] The statute defines foreign principal to include (1) foreign governments and foreign political parties; (2) persons outside the United States unless it is determined that the person is an individual and a citizen of and domiciled within the United States or that the person is not an individual and is organized under or created by the laws of the United States or a state and has its principal place of business within the United States; and (3) a business organized under the laws of or having its principal place of business in a foreign country.[73] However, agent of a foreign principal does not include any news or press service or association which is a corporation organized under United States or state law or any newspaper, magazine, periodical, or other publication having on file with the United States Postal Service required information so long as it is at least 80% beneficially owned by United States citizens, its officers and directors are all United States citizens, and the news or service or association, newspaper, magazine, periodical, or other publication is not owned, controlled, subsidized, or financed and none of its policies is determined by a foreign principal or its agent.[74]

Banking

The Bank Holding Company Act (BHCA)[75] regulates as a bank holding company (BHC) any company that controls a United States bank; i.e., a bank chartered by a state or the federal government to do banking in the United States (as distinguished from a foreign bank—a bank chartered by a foreign government and doing business in the United States pursuant to the terms of the International Banking Act of 1978[76]). "Control" of a bank or BHC is defined in terms of: (1) acquiring a 25% share or more of any class of voting securities of a bank or a BHC; (2) controlling the election of a majority of the directors or trustees of the bank or BHC; or (3) having been determined by the Board of Governors of the Federal Reserve System (FRB) to be exercising a controlling influence over the management or policies of the bank or BHC.[77]

The BHCA is administered by the FRB, which must solicit the "views and recommendations" of the Comptroller of the Currency for national bank acquisitions and the appropriate state bank supervisor for state-chartered bank acquisitions.[78]

The BHCA presumes that "any company which owns, controls, or has power to vote less than 5 per centum of any class of voting securities of a given bank or [bank holding] company does not have control over that bank or company."[79] Before any company may take any action which would cause that company to become a BHC or before any BHC may acquire a 5% share or more of the voting stock of any U.S. bank or BHC, it must seek approval from the FRB.[80] FRB's implementing regulation makes this requirement applicable to "foreign banking organizations."[81]

The BHCA generally subjects BHCs to activity restrictions that essentially confine their portfolios to banking and financial services. Under the BHCA, subject to specified, limited exceptions, any company which controls a bank may engage only in banking or managing or controlling banks and subsidiaries; specified, limited non-banking activities; and activities that are financial in nature or incidental to such financial activity as determined by the FRB and the Secretary of the Treasury. Permissible banking activities are found in Section 4(k) of the BHCA.[82] A list of permissible non-banking activities for BHCs is found at 12 C.F.R. Section 225.28. A further list of permissible non-banking activities for BHCs which have qualified as Financial Holding Companies under Section 4(l)(1) of the BHCA is found at 12 C.F.R. Section 225.86. In addition, the FRB has promulgated individual orders under the BHCA determining that particular activities are "so closely related to banking as to be a proper incident thereto."[83]

The BHCA's Section 2(h)(2) states that a foreign company that acquires stock of a U.S. bank or BHC is not subject to BHCA activities restrictions if: (1) it is organized as a bank holding company under foreign law and is principally engaged in the banking business outside of the United States.[84] A further provision states that nothing in the preceding provision authorizes such a foreign company to hold more than 5% of the outstanding shares of any class of voting securities of a company engaged in banking, securities, insurance, or other financial activities, as defined by the Federal Reserve Board, in the United States.[85] There is also authority for the Federal Reserve Board to provide a foreign company which acquires the stock of a U.S. bank or BHC an exemption from the activities restrictions if the Federal Reserve Board determines "by regulation or order ... under circumstances and subject to the conditions set forth in the regulation or order, [that] the exemption would not be substantially at variance with purposes of [the BHCA] ... and would be in the public interest."[86]

Government Contracting

Corporations which are controlled or owned by foreign citizens can conduct business with the federal government on generally the same basis as domestic corporations which are owned completely by United States citizens. However, some federal statutes restrict purchases of products by federal agencies to those manufactured in the United States.

For example, American materials may be required for public use.

> Only unmanufactured articles, materials, and supplies that have been mined or produced in the United states, and only manufactured articles, materials, and supplies that have been manufactured in the United States substantially all from articles, materials, or supplies mined, produced, or manufactured in the United States, shall be acquired for public use unless the head of the department or independent establishment concerned determines their acquisition to be inconsistent with the public interest or their cost to be unreasonable.[87]

Every contract for the construction or repair of a public building or public work shall have a provision that the contractor or supplier shall use only unmanufactured articles or materials mined or produced in the United States.[88]

Some exceptions should be noted. For example, the Trade Agreements Act of 1979[89] gives the President the authority to waive application of foreign citizen restrictions on the products of our trading partners. However, this does not authorize the waiver of any small business or minority preference.[90]

No entity controlled by a foreign government is allowed to merge with, acquire, or take over a company engaged in interstate commerce in the United States which is performing a Department of Defense (DOD) contract or a Department of Energy (DOE) contract under a national security program that cannot be performed satisfactorily unless that company is given access to information in a proscribed category of information. Such a merger, acquisition or takeover is also not allowed to occur if the company engaged in interstate commerce in the United States was during the previous fiscal year awarded Department of Defense prime contracts in an aggregate amount exceeding $500 million or Department of Energy prime contracts under national security programs exceeding $500 million.[91] This limitation shall not apply if the merger, acquisition, or takeover is not suspended or prohibited under the statutes carried out by the Committee on Foreign Investment in the United States, as discussed below.[92]

Investment Company Regulation

The Investment Company Act of 1940[93] requires registration with the Securities and Exchange Commission (SEC) of an investment company which does business in the United States. Only investment companies organized or created under the laws of the United States or a state are allowed to sell their own securities in interstate commerce in connection with a public offering unless the SEC finds that it is legally and practically feasible to enforce the federal securities laws against the investment company and that the exemption from registration is consistent with the public interest and the protection of investors.[94]

The Trust Indenture Act of 1939[95] prohibits the sale in interstate commerce of certain securities which have not been registered under the Securities Act of 1933 unless the securities have been issued under an indenture.[96] There must be at least one or more trustees under the indenture, at least one of whom shall be a corporation organized and doing business under the laws of the United States, a state, territory, or the District of Columbia or a corporation or other person permitted to act as trustee by the SEC which is authorized to exercise corporate trust powers and is subject to supervision or examination by federal, state, territorial, or District of Columbia authority.[97]

COMMITTEE ON FOREIGN INVESTMENT IN THE UNITED STATES[98]

The Committee on Foreign Investment in the United States (CFIUS) is a multi-member board headed by the Secretary of the Treasury.[99] CFIUS may review any "covered transaction," defined as any merger, acquisition, or takeover by or with a foreign person which could result in foreign control of any person engaged in interstate commerce in the United States,[100] for its possible impact upon national security. Factors to be considered in determining the impact upon national security are numerous and include domestic production needed for projected national defense requirements, the capability and capacity of domestic industries to meet national defense requirements, the control of domestic industries and commercial activity by foreign citizens as it affects the capability and capacity of the United States to meet the requirements of national security, and the potential effects of the proposed or pending transaction on United States international technological leadership in areas affecting United States national security.[101] If the Committee determines that the acquiring party is an entity controlled by a foreign government, the Committee shall conduct an investigation of the transaction as a national security investigation.[102]

End Notes

[1] *See, e.g.*, Bouve, EXCLUSION AND EXPULSION OF ALIENS IN THE UNITED STATES 3 (1912); *United States ex rel. Knauff* v. *Shaughnessy*, 338 U.S. 537 (1950); and *The Schooner Exchange* v. *McFaddon*, 11 U.S. (7 Cranch) 116 (1812).

[2] tolt: In Old English law, a writ whereby a cause depending in a court baron was taken and removed into a county court. BLACK'S LAW DICTIONARY (6th ed. 1990).

[3] Nussbaum, A CONCISE HISTORY OF THE LAW OF NATIONS 27 (1954).

[4] Much of this historical discussion is based on chapter 1 of A GUIDE TO FOREIGN INVESTMENT UNDER UNITED STATES LAW by the Committee to Study Foreign Investment in the United States of the Section of Corporation, Banking and Business Law of the American Bar Association (New York 1979).

[5] 3 Annals of Congress 994 (1791).

[6] Boorstin, *Foreign Investments in America*, 2 Editorial Research Reports 572-573 (1974).

[7] A creditor nation may be defined as a country which exports more than it imports; a debtor nation imports more than it exports. A creditor nation may also be defined as a country whose domestic savings are greater than its domestic investment; a debtor nation is a country whose domestic savings are less than its domestic investment.

[8] Act of March 3, 1887, ch. 340, §1, 24 Stat. 476.

[9] Art. I, §8, cl. 4.

[10] Art. I, §8, cl. 3.

[11] Art. I, §8, cl. 12.

[12] *Chinese Exclusion Case (Chae Chan Ping)* v. *United States*, 130 U.S. 581, 603-604 (1889).

[13] *See Fiallo* v. *Bell*, 430 U.S. 787 (1977).

[14] Art. I, §8, cl. 3.

[15] *See, e.g., North American Company* v. *Securities and Exchange Commission*, 327 U.S. 686 (1946); and *Electric Bond Company* v. *Securities and Exchange Commission*, 303 U.S. 419 (1938).

[16] 389 U.S. 429 (1967).

[17] *Id.*, at 434.

[18] Note, *United States Regulation of Foreign Direct Investment: Current Developments and the Congressional Response*, 15 VA. J. INT'L L. 611, 621 (1975).

[19] *See Plyler* v. *Doe*, 457 U.S. 202 (1982).

[20] 403 U.S. 365 (1971).

[21] *Id.*, at 371.

[22] *Takahashi* v. *Fish and Game Commission*, 334 U.S. 410 (1948).

[23] *In Re Griffiths*, 413 U.S. 717 (1973).

[24] *Sugarman* v. *Dougall*, 413 U.S. 634 (1973).

[25] *Nyquist* v. *Mauclet*, 432 U.S. 1 (1977).

[26] *Foley* v. *Connelie*, 435 U.S. 291 (1978).

[27] *Ambash* v. *Norwich*, 441 U.S. 68 (1979).

[28] It is also possible that nonresident aliens, such as a Japanese bank doing business in the United States, are entitled to the same degree of equal protection under the Fourteenth Amendment as resident aliens, but this is an issue which appears not to have been settled by the courts.

With respect, however, to actions by the federal government, it appears clear that Congress can discriminate against nonresident aliens so long as the restriction is reasonable and does not violate their procedural rights. *See, e.g.*, statutes discussed later in this report. No major cases challenging their constitutionality were found.

[29] *Mathews* v. *Diaz*, 426 U.S. 67, 81 (1975).
[30] *Id.*
[31] *Kleindienst* v. *Mandel*, 408 U.S. 753 (1972).
[32] *See Chinese Exclusion Case (Chae Chan Ping)* v. *United States*, 130 U.S. 581, 603-604 (1889).
[33] 22 U.S.C. §§3101 *et seq.*
[34] 22 U.S.C. §3101(b).
[35] E.O. 11961 (January 19, 1977), 42 Fed. Reg. 4321.
[36] 22 U.S.C. §3103(b).
[37] 22 U.S.C. §3103(a)(5).
[38] 22 U.S.C. §3103(h).
[39] 22 U.S.C. §§3141 *et seq.*
[40] S.Rept. 101-443, 101st Cong., 2d Sess. 1 (August 30, 1990).
[41] 22 U.S.C. §§3142 and 3143.
[42] 13 U.S.C. §402.
[43] 7 U.S.C. §§3501 *et seq.*
[44] 7 U.S.C. §3501(a).
[45] 7 U.S.C. §3501(b).
[46] P.L. 95-213.
[47] 15 U.S.C. §78m(d).
[48] Hearings on S. 245, the Foreign Investment Act of 1975 Before the Subcomm. on Securities of the Senate Comm. on Banking, Housing, and Urban Affairs, 94th Cong., 1st Sess. (1975).
[49] 46 U.S.C. §12102(a).
[50] 49 U.S.C. §44101.
[51] 49 U.S.C. §44102.
[52] 49 U.S.C. §40102(a)(15).
[53] 49 U.S.C. §41703.
[54] 49 U.S.C. §44711.
[55] 49 U.S.C. §44703(e).
[56] 49 U.S.C. §§44301 *et seq.*
[57] 49 U.S.C. §44303.
[58] 30 U.S.C. §22.
[59] 30 U.S.C. §24.
[60] 30 U.S.C. §181.
[61] 43 U.S.C. §§1331 *et seq.*
[62] 30 C.F.R. §256.35.
[63] 16 U.S.C. §797(e).
[64] 42 U.S.C. §2133(d).
[65] Ch. LXXV, §1, Stat. 392 (1862).
[66] 43 U.S.C. §321.
[67] 43 U.S.C. §315b.
[68] 43 U.S.C. §375.
[69] 47 U.S.C. §310(a).
[70] 47 U.S.C. §310(b).
[71] 22 U.S.C. §§611 *et seq.*
[72] 22 U.S.C. §614.
[73] 22 U.S.C. §611.
[74] 22 U.S.C. §611(d).
[75] 12 U.S.C. §§1841-1849.
[76] 12 U.S.C. §§3101-3111.

[77] 12 U.S.C. §1841(a)(2).
[78] 12 U.S.C. §1842(b)(1).
[79] 12 U.S.C. §1841(a)(3).
[80] 12 U.S.C. §1842; 12 C.F.R. §225.11.
[81] 12 C.F.R. §225.11(f).
[82] 12 U.S.C. §1843(k).
[83] *See, e.g.,* Order Approving a Notice to Engage in Real Estate Title Abstracting, The First National Company, Storm Lake, Iowa, effective June 30, 1995, 81 FRB 805 (August 1993); Order Approving the Acquisition of a Title Insurance Agency, Norwest Corporation, Minneapolis, Minnesota, effective March 8, 1993, 79 FRB 517 (May 1993); and Order Approving the Acquisition of a Title Insurance Agency, Norwest Corporation, Minneapolis, Minnesota, effective October 15, 1990, 76 FRB 1058 (December 1990).
[84] 12 U.S.C. §1841(h)(2).
[85] 12 U.S.C. §1841(h)(3).
[86] 12 U.S.C. §1843(c)(9).
[87] 41 U.S.C. §8302(a).
[88] 41 U.S.C. §8303(a).
[89] 19 U.S.C. §§2501 *et seq.*
[90] 19 U.S.C. §2511.
[91] 50 U.S.C. App. §2170a(a).
[92] 50 U.S.C. App. §2170a(b).
[93] 15 U.S.C. §§80a-1 *et seq.*
[94] 15 U.S.C. §80a-7(d).
[95] 15 U.S.C. §§77aaa *et seq.*
[96] 15 U.S.C. §77fff(a).
[97] 15 U.S.C. §77jjj(a)(1).
[98] For details about CFIUS and about policy issues, *see* CRS Report RL33388, *The Committee on Foreign Investment in the United States (CFIUS)*, by James K. Jackson.
[99] 50 U.S.C. App. §2170.
[100] 50 U.S.C. App. §2170(a).
[101] 50 U.S.C. App. §2170(f).
[102] 50 U.S.C. App. §2170(b)(1)(B).

In: Foreign Investment in the U.S.
Editor: Theodore L. Newell
ISBN: 978-1-62948-930-8

Chapter 4

FOREIGN INVESTMENT AND NATIONAL SECURITY: ECONOMIC CONSIDERATIONS*

James K. Jackson

SUMMARY

The United States is the largest foreign direct investor in the world and also the largest recipient of foreign direct investment. This dual role means that globalization, or the spread of economic activity by firms across national borders, has become a prominent feature of the U.S. economy and that through direct investment the U.S. economy has become highly enmeshed with the broader global economy. This also means that the United States has important economic, political, and social interests at stake in the development of international policies regarding direct investment. With some exceptions for national security, the United States has established domestic policies that treat foreign investors no less favorably than U.S. firms.

The terrorist attacks on the United States on September 11, 2001, spurred some Members of Congress and others to call for a reexamination of elements of the traditionally open environment in the United States for foreign investment. In particular, some Members argue that greater consideration must be given to the long-term impact of foreign direct investment on the structure and the industrial capacity of the economy and on the ability of the economy

* This is an edited, reformatted and augmented version of the Congressional Research Service Publication, CRS Report for Congress RL34561, dated April 4, 2013.

to meet the needs of U.S. defense and security interests. In addition, policymakers from a broad group of nations are evaluating their national policies concerning foreign investment within the context of their national security concerns. As a result of these initiatives, Members of Congress may be pressed to address U.S. policies that focus on the role of foreign direct investment more extensively within a broader national security framework.

This report assesses recent international developments as the leaders from a number of nations work to reach a consensus on an informal set of best practices regarding national restrictions on foreign investment for national security purposes. This report also provides one possible approach for assessing the costs and benefits involved in using national policies to direct or to restrict foreign direct investment for national security reasons. Within the United States, there is no consensus yet among Members of Congress or between the Congress and the Administration over a working set of parameters that establishes a functional definition of the national economic security implications of foreign direct investment. In part, this issue reflects differing assessments of the economic impact of foreign investment on the U.S. economy and differing political and philosophical convictions among Members and between the Congress and the Administration.

OVERVIEW

For more than half a century, the United States has led international efforts to reduce restrictions on foreign investment. In part, these efforts are related to a general commitment to open markets and to the free flow of international capital as an important component in economic development. At the same time, the United States is the largest foreign direct investor in the world and also the largest recipient of foreign direct investment. By year-end 2011, foreign direct investment in the United States had reached $2.6 trillion and U.S. direct investment abroad had reached $4.1 trillion, when direct investment is measured at historical cost. This dual role means that globalization, or the spread of economic activity by firms across national borders, has become a prominent feature of the U.S. economy and that through direct investment the U.S. economy has become highly enmeshed with the broader global economy.

The globalization of the economy also means that the United States has important economic, political, and social interests at stake in the development of international policies regarding direct investment. With some exceptions for national security,[1] the United States has established domestic policies that treat foreign investors no less favorably than U.S. firms. In addition, the United States has led efforts over the past 50 years to negotiate internationally for reduced restrictions on foreign direct investment, for greater controls over incentives offered to foreign investors, and for equal treatment under law of foreign and domestic investors.

In light of the terrorist attacks on the United States on September 11, 2001, however, some Members of Congress have been reexamining some elements of this open-door policy and have argued for greater consideration of the long-term impact of foreign direct investment, especially where that investment takes the form of an acquisition, a merger, or a take-over of an existing U.S. company. In particular, these concerns have centered around the impact of such investments on the structure and the industrial capacity of the economy, and on the ability of the economy to meet the needs of U.S. defense and security interests, including a terrorist attack. As a result of these concerns, in 2007 Congress changed the way foreign direct investments are reviewed through P.L. 110-49, the Foreign Investment and National Security Act of 2007.[2] Through P.L. 110-49, Congress strengthened its role in reviewing foreign investments by enhancing its oversight capabilities. There is no precise way, however, to estimate the exact dollar amount for the economic costs and benefits of national policies that attempt to direct or restrict foreign direct investment for national security concerns. Also, there is no way to determine if foreign investment policies are implemented to enhance national security or to engage in a form of economic protectionism. In some cases, other policy tools may well be preferred over intervening in the foreign investment process.

FOREIGN DIRECT INVESTMENT IN THE UNITED STATES

Foreigners invested $234 billion in nominal terms in U.S. businesses and real estate in 2011, according to data published by the Department of Commerce.[3] As **Figure 1** shows, this represents a 14% increase over the $155 billion invested in 2010. Investments abroad by U.S. parent firms increased by 28% in 2011 to $419 billion, up from the $328 billion they invested abroad in 2010. The increase in foreign direct investment flows mirrors a rebound in global flows following the sharp drop in direct investment flows in 2009 and 2010. The cumulative amount, or stock, of foreign direct investment in the United States on a historical cost basis[4] rose from $2.26 trillion in 2010 to about \$2.55 trillion in 2011. This marked an increase of 12.5%.[5] The Department of Commerce does not attempt to deflate the annual nominal amounts for direct investment with a specific price deflator. Instead, the department publishes alternative estimates based on current cost and market value to provide other measures of the value of direct investment.

Foreign direct investments in the U.S. manufacturing sector as a whole in 2011 were higher than in 2010 and accounted for nearly half of the overall increase in foreign direct investment in 2011. Foreign direct investment in the banking, finance, retail trade, and professional services all increased in 2011, compared with investments in 2010. In comparison, investments were down in the wholesale trade, real estate, and information sectors. Data for the first two quarters of 2012 indicate that foreign direct investment in the United States is down about 41% from the amount recorded in the comparable period in 2011. Such investments may well continue to lag behind similar investment in 2010 in the second half of the year if the rate of economic growth stalls.

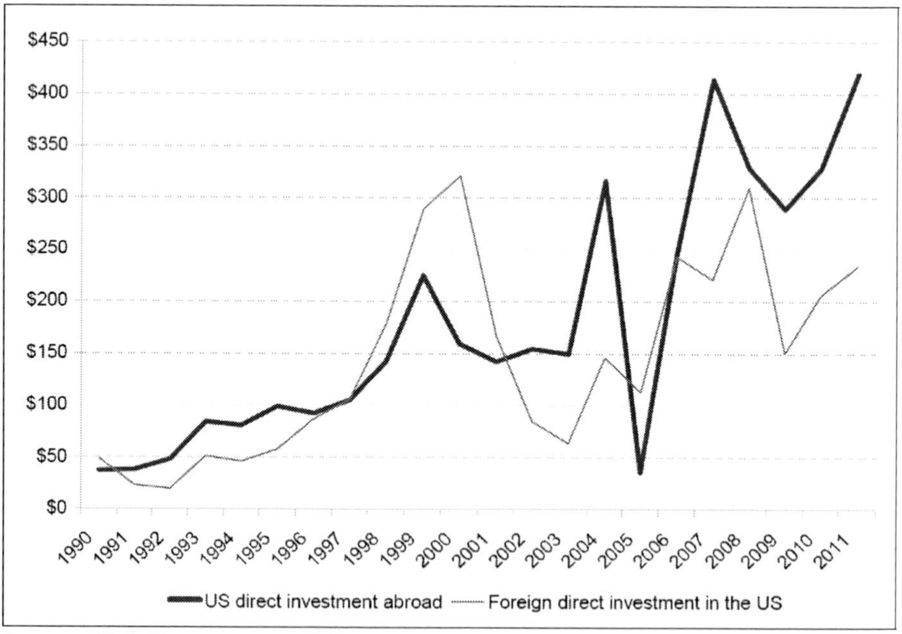

Source: U.S. Department of Commerce.

Note: The drop in U.S. direct investment abroad in 2005 reflects actions by U.S. parent companies to take advantage of a one-time tax provision.

Figure 1. Foreign Direct Investment in the United States and U.S. Direct Investment Abroad, Annual Flows, 1990-2011.

New spending by U.S. firms on businesses and real estate abroad, or U.S. direct investment abroad,[6] although substantial, fell sharply in 2009 compared to 2008. Net investments fell from $332 billion in 2008 to $221 billion in 2009, according to the Department of Commerce.[7] As indicated in **Figure 1**, a drop in U.S. direct investment abroad that occurred in 2005 reflects actions by U.S. parent firms to reduce the amount of reinvested earnings going to their foreign affiliates for distribution to the U.S. parent firms in order to take advantage of one-time tax provisions in the American Jobs Creation Act of 2004 (P.L. 108-357).

Table 1. Global Annual Inflows of Foreign Direct Investment, by Major Area (in billions of dollars and percent shares)

	2009	2010	2011	2009	2010	2011
	Inflows of foreign direct investment (in billions of dollars)			Share of annual foreign direct investment inflows (in percent)		
World	$1,197.8	$1,309.0	$1,524.4	100.0%	100.0%	100.0%
Developed economies	606.2	618.6	747.9	50.6	47.3	49.1
Western Europe	398.9	256.6	425.3	33.3	27.2	27.9
European Union	356.6	318.3	420.7	29.8	24.3	27.6
Other Western Europe	42.3	28.3	4.6	3.5	2.9	0.3
North America	165.0	221.3	267.9	13.8	16.9	17.6
United States	143.6	197.9	226.9	12.0	15.1	14.9
Other developed econ.	42.3	40.7	54.7	3.5	3.1	3.6
Developing economies	519.2	616.7	684.4	43.3	47.1	44.9
Africa	52.6	43.1	42.7	4.4	3.3	2.8
Latin America	149.4	187.4	217.0	12.5	14.3	14.2
Asia	315.2	384.1	423.2	26.3	29.3	27.8
Other Europe	72.4	73.8	92.2	6.0	5.6	6.0

Source: *World Investment Report, 2010*, United Nations. Annex table B.1, 2012.

According to the U.N. *World Investment Report*,[8] global foreign investment flows reached $1.5 trillion in 2011, a 16% increase over the amount recorded in 2010 in 2011, as indicated in **Table 1**. The growth in foreign investment flows reflects higher profits by multinational corporations and an increase in the rate of growth in developing countries. In 2009, global foreign investment flows dropped by 33% from that recorded in 2008, reflecting the financial crisis and drop in economic growth in most developed economies. The developed economies traditionally have absorbed about two-thirds of global direct investment flows, but this share dropped to half between 2009 and 2011, reflecting the differential impact of the financial crisis which affected the developed economies more than the developing economies. Africa continues to receive the smallest share, generally less than 5%, with Latin America receiving about 14% and Asia getting close to one-third during the 2009-2011 period. A study on investment trends by the Organization for Economic Cooperation and Development (OECD) reported that direct investment outflows reached a record $1.8 trillion in 2007, in part due the decline in the value of the dollar relative to the Euro, which results in an upward valuation in dollar terms in investments that originally had been priced in Euros.

Globally, the total, or cumulative, amount of foreign direct investment surpassed $20 trillion in 2011 (the latest year for which detailed data are available), as indicated in **Figure 2**. Nearly three- fourths of this amount is invested in the most economically-advanced developed economies. The developed economies as a group not only are the largest recipient of investment funds, but they are also the largest source of those funds. Similar to the United States, those countries that are the largest overseas investors also tend to be the most attractive destinations for foreign investments. The clear exception to this general observation is Japan, which had invested $962 billion abroad through 2011, but had received $226 billion in investment inflows. Among the developing economies, Asia, which includes China, had accumulated $4.0 trillion in direct investment, followed by Latin America (2.05 trillion) and Africa ($570 billion).

By the end of 2010, there were about 2,300 U.S. parent companies with nearly 27,000 affiliates operating abroad, as **Table 2** indicates. In comparison, foreign firms had about 6,000 affiliates operating in the United States. U.S. parent companies employed nearly 23 million workers in the United States, compared with the 13.3 million workers employed abroad by U.S. firms and the 5.8 million persons employed in the United States by foreign firms. Although the U.S.-based affiliates of foreign firms employ less than half as many workers as the foreign affiliates of U.S. firms, they paid about 80% of the aggregate employee compensation in the United States as did the U.S. affiliates operating abroad. The affiliates of foreign firms operating in the United States had a higher value of gross product than did the foreign affiliates of U.S. parent companies. The foreign affiliates of U.S. firms, however, had total sales that were nearly twice as high as those of the U.S. affiliates of foreign firms. The foreign affiliates of U.S. firms, however, paid 10 times more in taxes to foreign governments than the affiliates of foreign firms operating in the United States paid in taxes to the U.S. government.

U.S. multinational companies also play an important role in the U.S. economy. According to the total output of U.S. parent companies, or gross product, they produced $2.9 trillion in goods and services in 2010, up 21% from the $2.4 trillion dollars they produced in 2009. This amount comprised about 21% of total U.S. private industry gross product, a share of total gross product of U.S. parent companies that has remained fairly consistent since the early 1990s despite significant changes in the U.S. economy as a whole. The data also demonstrate the impact the improvement in the U.S. economy after 2002 had on the operations of U.S. multinational companies.

Table 2. Select Data on U.S. Multinational Companies and on Foreign Firms Operating in the United States, 2010 (in millions of dollars unless otherwise indicated)

	U.S. Multinational Companies		U.S. Affiliates of Foreign Firms
	Parent Companies	Affiliates	
Number of firms	2,302	26,791	6,062
Employment (thousands)	22,820	13,256	5,802
Employee compensation	$1,612,953	$552,627	$440,756
Gross product	$2,885,927	$1,241,272	$1,780,699
Total assets	$29,508,242	$23,277,276	$12,337,290
Sales	$9,772,683	$6,034,813	$3,400,736
Taxes	$203,011	$209,605	$15,419
R&D Expenditures	$212,513	$39,470	$45,251

Source: *U.S. Direct Investment Abroad: Operations of U.S. Parent Companies and Their Foreign Affiliates, Preliminary 2010 Estimates; and Foreign Direct Investment in the United States: Operations of U.S. Affiliates of Foreign Companies, Preliminary 2010 Estimates.*

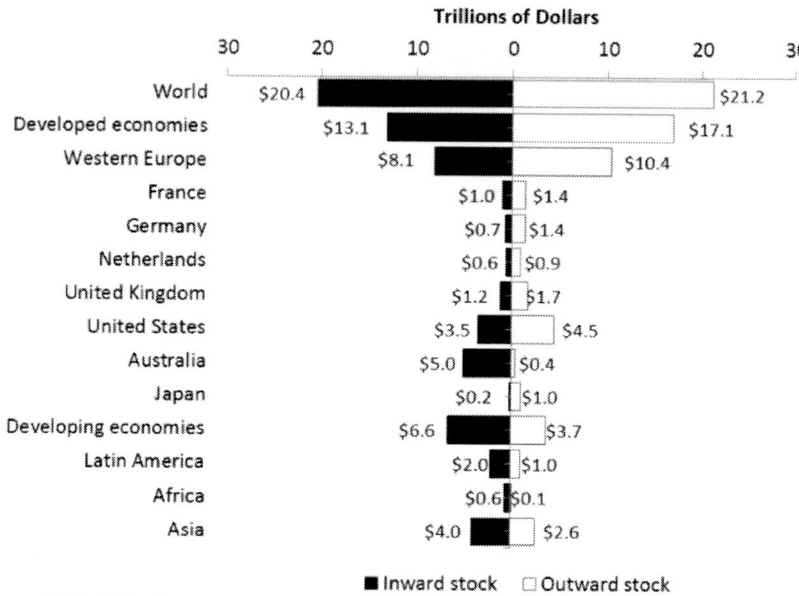

Source: United Nations.

Figure 2. Inward and Outward Global Direct Investment Position, by Major Area, 2011.

NATIONAL SECURITY

Since the end of World War II, the United States has led efforts internationally to reduce official government restrictions on foreign investment. One prominent exclusion to these efforts and to commitments incorporated in international treaties is the right of nations to protect their own "essential security interests." The terrorist attacks of September 11, 2001, combined with the growing role of state-backed investors, or sovereign wealth funds (SWFs),[9] has spurred a number of nations to reconsider their national security interests relative to inward investment and to consider placing additional restrictions on foreign investments in areas considered to be an essential security interest.[10] For the most part, such restrictions apply to mergers, acquisitions, and takeovers of existing firms and not generally to new establishments. These actions, in turn, have raised concerns among the members of such organizations as the OECD,[11] which promotes the concept of liberalized government restrictions on the free flow of international investment.

OECD Arrangements

With some exceptions for national security, the United States has long been considered one of the most receptive economies in the world to foreign direct investment. The United States has led efforts to negotiate internationally for reduced restrictions on foreign direct investment, for greater rules on incentives offered to foreign investors, and for equal treatment under law of foreign and domestic investors. In particular, the United States has supported efforts within the OECD to develop such legally non-binding arrangements as the OECD Code of Liberalization of Capital Movements (covering both long- and short-term capital movements) and the Code of Liberalization of Current Invisible Operations (covering cross-border trade in services). In addition, the OECD has issued a basic statement on foreign investment, *The Declaration on International Investment and Multinational Enterprises*, which is a general statement of policy regarding the rights and responsibilities of foreign investors.

The United States and other signatories to the OECD arrangements recognize that one notable exception to the open investment policies provided for in the OECD instruments, as well as in customary international law, is that governments can take measures they "consider necessary to protect essential security interests" and to maintain "public order or the protection of public health, morals, and safety." Such an exception has been recognized in various international agreements, in countless bilateral investment treaties, and in investment chapters of free trade agreements. According to the OECD, "The right to protect essential security interests of the state, as an exception to treaty commitments, has been well established in treaty practice."[12]

Another aspect of this policy is that each state is best situated to assess its own security interests and to decide whether essential security interests are at stake relative to certain types of investments. Under customary international law, the argument of necessity has been interpreted to mean an incident that poses a grave and imminent peril to a country, or a threat to such vital interests as, "political or economic survival, the continued functioning of its essential services, the maintenance of internal peace, the survival of a sector of its population, and the preservation of the environment of its territory."[13] Various agreements, including multilateral agreements and OECD investment instruments, acknowledge that each nation has the exclusive role of determining for itself whether a restriction on foreign investment is necessary to protect its essential security interests.

As governments move to assess their national policies on foreign investments, they are faced with a trade-off between their desires to preserve and expand an open international investment environment with the national responsibility to safeguard essential security interests. This trade- off is complicated further by the nature of the threats that are associated with mergers, acquisitions, and takeovers of existing firms. Such investments generally are not viewed as posing an immediate threat to the stability or security of a nation. Some observers, however, view some of these investments as posing potential threats to the economy in the form of a loss of technology related to national security, a loss of jobs due to outsourcing, or a threat associated with state-backed investors who use their investments to advance political objectives. As a result, policies directed at reviewing foreign direct investments are best described as precautionary measures.[14] In this report, the national security threats posed by mergers, acquisition, or takeovers do not include overt acts of transnational terrorism that are meant to dissuade foreign capital inflows.[15] The OECD reports that a number of governments have started to review their policies on inward foreign investment in response to a "changing context for national security and the increasing prominence of new investors, including large investors controlled by foreign governments."[16] From France and Germany, the United States and Canada, to various non-OECD countries, existing regulatory regimes have been used to deter certain investments in infrastructure for national security concerns or countries have tightened their regulations on security grounds.[17]

Due to the increased attention focused on the national security aspects of inward foreign investment, the OECD formed in June 2006 the "Freedom of Investment, National Security and 'Strategic Industries'" project. Through the 13 rounds of meetings, including the latest one held in October 2010, members[18] of the investment project have agreed to support three principles for national investment policy measures that address essential security interests: (1) transparency and predictability;[19] (2) proportionality;[20] and (3) accountability. Proportionality refers to the concept that restrictions on foreign investment should be no greater than is needed to protect national security. In June 2007 at the annual summit of the Group of Eight[21] (G8) leading industrialized nations, the group issued a "Declaration on Freedom of Investment, Environment and Social Responsibility." The final summit statement also emphasized the group's continuing support for the OECD project on Freedom of Investment, National Security and "Strategic Industries." The G8 statement also offered its support for a free flow of investment by indicating that

> We will work together to strengthen open and transparent investment regimes and to fight against tendencies to restrict them. Erecting barriers and supporting protectionism would result in a loss of prosperity. We therefore agree on the central role of free and open markets to facilitate global capital movements. We reaffirm that freedom of investment is a crucial pillar of economic growth, prosperity and employment.... Against this background we remain committed to minimize any national restrictions on foreign investment. Such restrictions should apply to very limited cases which primarily concern national security. The general principles to be followed in such cases are non-discrimination, transparency and predictability. In any case, restrictive measures should not exceed the necessary scope, intensity and duration.[22]

The OECD project on investment issued its final report in mid-2009 titled, "Building Trust and Confidence in International Investment," which included policy guidance in the form of a menu of best practices for the signatories to consider so that as they implement investment policies they do so in a way that is consistent with the three principles. So far, a number of OECD nations, including the United States, have adjusted their national laws to have them conform to the recommendations of the OECD's final report. At the Toronto Summit of the G-20 nations in June 2010, the members tasked the OECD with reporting on the trade and investment measures of the G-20 members. The recent OECD report indicated that G-20 members had resisted protectionist pressures and had taken measures aimed at facilitating and encouraging investment flows, but none of the OECD members had not adopted new restrictions on foreign investment related to national security.[23] The OECD members have agreed to adopt a set of 14 guidelines that are meant to serve as the basis for establishing investment policy measures. These guidelines are designed to assist nations in adopting investment measures that safeguard national security and are consistent with the three principles of transparency, proportionality, and accountability. These measures are:

- Non-discrimination: Governments should treat similarly situated foreign and domestic investments in a similar fashion.
- Transparency/Predictability: Regulatory practices should be as transparent as possible while also protecting the confidentiality of sensitive information.
- Codification and publication: Laws, particularly evaluation criteria used in reviews of investment transactions, should be codified and made public.

- Prior notification: Governments should take steps to notify interested parties about plans to change investment policies.
- Consultation: Governments should seek the views of interested parties when they are considering changing investment policies.
- Procedural fairness and predictability: Reviews should have time limits; sensitive information should be protected.
- Disclosure of investment policy actions: Governments should disclose investment policy actions as a measure of accountability.
- Regulatory proportionality: Restrictions should not be greater than needed to protect national security.
- Essential security concerns are self-judging: Countries have the right to determine what is necessary to protect their own national security.
- Narrow focus: Investment restrictions should be narrowly focused on concerns related to national security.
- Appropriate expertise: Measures related to national security concerns should be designed so that they can benefit from national expertise on national security and that it is possible to weigh the benefits of the investment policies against the impact of the restrictions.
- Tailored responses: Investment measures should be tailored to the specific risks posed by specific investment proposals.
- Last resort: Restrictive investment should be used as a last resort when other policies cannot be used to eliminate security-related concerns.
- Accountability: To ensure accountability by government agencies, investment measures should be reviewed by government oversight, judicial review, periodic regulatory impact assessments, and requirements that decisions to block an investment should be taken at high government levels.

Critical Infrastructure

As part of the general area of essential security concerns associated with foreign investment, numerous nations have focused on the concept of critical infrastructure as a separate area of concern within the rubric of essential security interests.[24] As **Table 3** indicates, national definitions of critical infrastructure differ among countries, although most of the countries surveyed by the OECD define critical infrastructure as physical infrastructure that provides essential support for economic and social well-being, for public safety, and for the functioning of key government responsibilities. In most cases, the national definitions of critical infrastructure are broad statements that provide national governments with a wide latitude for deciding which assets or sectors to designate as critical. Such definitions implicitly acknowledge the importance that the broader economic and security context plays in determining which sectors might be selected for designation as critical and that this designation may change depending on the circumstances.

Table 3. Examples of National Definitions of Critical Infrastructure

Australia	Those physical facilities, supply chains, information technologies and communication networks which, if destroyed, degraded or rendered unavailable for an extended period, would significantly impact on the social or economic well-being of the nation, or affect Australia's ability to conduct national defense and ensure national security.
Canada	Those physical and information technology facilities, networks, services and assets which, if disrupted or destroyed, would have a serious impact on the health, safety, security or economic well-being of Canadians or the effective functioning of governments in Canada.
Germany	Organizations and facilities of major importance to the community whose failure or impairment would cause a sustained shortage of supplies, significant disruptions to public order or other dramatic consequences.
Netherlands	Products, services and the accompanying processes that, in the event of disruption or failure could cause major social disturbance. This could be in the form of tremendous casualties and severe economic damage.
United Kingdom	Those assets, services and systems that support the economic, political and social life of the UK whose importance is such that loss could: (1) cause large-scale loss of life; (2) have a serious impact on the national security; (3) have other grave social consequences for the community; or (4) be of immediate concern to the national government.
United States	In the overall U.S. critical infrastructure plan the definition includes systems and assets, whether physical or virtual, so vital to the United States that the incapacity or destruction of such systems and assets would have a debilitating impact on security, national economic security, national public health or safety, or any combination of those matters. For investment policy it is defined as: those systems and assets, whether physical or virtual, so vital to the United states that the incapacity or destruction of such systems and assets would have a debilitating impact on national security.

Source: *Protection of Critical Infrastructure and the Role of Investment Policies Relating to National Security*, The Organization for Economic Cooperation and Development, May 2008.

Essential Security Exclusions

Members of the OECD and other countries that choose to adhere to the voluntary OECD National Treatment Instrument retain the option to exclude sectors of their economy on the grounds of essential security interests from the national treatment standard. In such cases, nations are using discriminatory practices to restrict foreigners from investing in sectors of their economies that are deemed to be important to national security. In making such exceptions, nations that are parties to the National Treatment Instrument provide a notification to the other members that they are requesting an exemption from the protocol, thereby providing a method to make the process transparent to all the signatories of the Instrument.

According to a recent OECD study, countries that are adhering to the OECD National Treatment Instrument have exempted an extensive array of discriminatory foreign investment policies from the Instrument in order to protect critical infrastructure from foreign investment. For instance, all 39 nations that are a party to the Instrument report that they discriminate against foreign investment in one or more critical infrastructure sectors. Of these sectors, transport in the most targeted sector, with all 39 countries reported having discriminatory measures.[25] Such restrictions generally fall within three categories: (1) blanket restrictions that cover a specific activity; (2) sector-specific restrictions that affect investment in a specific sector of the economy; and (3) measures that apply to a broad range of infrastructure investments and approval procedures that could be used to block infrastructure investments that are deemed to pose threats to essential security interests.

The OECD also concluded that the national restrictions were notably general in their descriptions. In turn, the OECD concluded that the generality of the restrictions is due to four issues: (1) the nature of the security threats may affect perceived threats and vulnerabilities; (2) the assessment of the threats may be affected by the nationality of the foreign investor; (3) some perceived threats may be resolved easily through mitigation efforts, while others may not; and (4) not all countries have the capabilities to conduct in-depth evaluations of potential national security threats. The OECD also concluded that it is difficult to assess the value such restrictions have in enhancing the essential national security of the members. In most cases, such policies are measures of last resort when other national laws or measures are determined to be insufficient, or they can provide a process that assists various agencies within a national government with identifying and dealing with security threats that might be posed by international investment.[26]

Table 4. Industrial Sectors Included in National Critical Infrastructure Plans

Sector	Australia	Canada	Netherlands	United Kingdom	United States	European Union
Energy (including nuclear)	X	X	X	X	X	X
Communications	X		X	X	X	X
Finance	X	X	X	X	X	X
Health care	X	X	X	X	X	X
Food	X	X	X	X	X	X
Water	X	X	X	X	X	X
Transport	X	X	X	X	X	X
Safety	Emergency services	X	X	Emergency services	Emergency services	X
Government		X	X	X	X	X
Chemicals		X	X		X	X
Defense industrial base	X	X	X		X	
Other sectors or activities	Public gatherings, national icons		Legal/ judicial		Dams, commercial facilities, national monuments	Space and research facilities

Source: *Protection of Critical Infrastructure and the Role of Investment Policies Relating to National Security*, The Organization for Economic Cooperation and Development, May 2008.

U.S. Foreign Investment Policy

U.S. policy toward foreign direct investment is based primarily on the conclusion that direct investment benefits both the home and the host country and that the benefits of such investment outweigh the costs. Most economists argue that free and unimpeded international flows of capital, such as direct investment, positively affect both the domestic (home) and foreign (host) economies. The essence of this argument is that for the home country, direct investment abroad benefits individual firms, because firms that invest abroad are better able to exploit their existing competitive advantages and are able to acquire additional skills and advantages. This tends to further enhance the competitive position of these firms both at home and abroad and shifts the composition and distribution of employment within the economy toward the most productive and efficient firms and away from the less productive firms.

As a host country, the United States benefits from inward direct investment, because the investment adds permanently to the Nation's capital stock and skill set. Direct investment also brings technological advances, since firms that invest abroad generally possess advanced technology, processes, and other economic advantages. Such investment also boosts capital formation, contributes to a growth in a competitive business environment and to productivity. In addition, direct investment contributes to international trade and integration into the global trading community, since most firms that invest abroad are established multinational firms.[27]

While U.S. policy toward inward and outward direct investment generally has adhered to the overall objective of treating such investment impartially, there are a number of notable exceptions. These exceptions can be classified as sectoral restrictions that exclude foreign ownership from certain sectors of the economy and approval procedures for mergers, acquisitions, and takeovers of existing U.S. firms that could be used to block infrastructure investments that are deemed to pose threats to essential national security. Foreign investors are constrained by U.S. laws that bars foreign ownership in such industrial sectors as maritime, aircraft, mining, energy, lands, communications, banking, and government contracting.[28] Generally, these sectors were closed to foreign investors to prevent public services and public interest activities from falling under foreign control, primarily for national defense purposes.

Exxon-Florio and CFIUS

The second category of restrictions, characterized by such approval procedures as the Exxon- Florio provision, applies to foreign investment in existing U.S. firms through mergers, acquisitions, or takeovers, but does not apply to foreign investors who establish new businesses. In 1988, Congress approved the Exxon-Florio provision[29] as part of the Omnibus Trade Act.[30] The Exxon-Florio provision grants the President broad discretionary authority to take what action he considers to be "appropriate" to suspend or prohibit proposed or pending foreign acquisitions, mergers, or takeovers "of persons engaged in interstate commerce in the United States" which "threaten to impair the national security." The Exxon-Florio provision does not define national security, because Congress meant to have the term interpreted broadly. Nevertheless, regulations developed by the Treasury Department to implement the law direct the members of the Committee on Foreign Investment in the United States (CFIUS)[31] to focus their reviews of foreign investments exclusively on those transactions that involve "products or key technologies essential to the U.S. defense industrial base," and not to consider economic concerns more broadly. CFIUS also indicated that in order to assure an unimpeded inflow of foreign investment it would implement the statute "only insofar as necessary to protect the national security," and "in a manner fully consistent with the international obligations of the United States."[32] The Committee is an interagency organization that serves the President in overseeing the national security implications of foreign investment in the economy.

The Exxon-Florio process consists of three different steps for reviewing proposed or pending foreign "mergers, acquisitions, or takeovers" of "persons engaged in interstate commerce in the United States" to determine if the transaction "threatens to impair the national security." Such investments often imply a change in ownership and not necessarily a change in the operations of the targeted U.S. company. CFIUS has 30 days to conduct a review, 45 days to conduct an investigation, and then the President has 15 days to make his determination. The President is the only officer with the authority to suspend or prohibit mergers, acquisitions, and takeovers.

Neither Congress nor the Administration have attempted to define the term national security as it appears in the Exxon-Florio statute. Treasury Department officials have indicated, however, that during a review or investigation each member of CFIUS is expected to apply that definition of national security that is consistent with the representative agency's specific legislative mandate.[33] For instance, over time and through a series of Executive Orders, the Department of Defense has developed the National Industrial Security Program (NISP) through which it has adopted various provisions under the term, "Foreign Ownership, Control, or Influence (FOCI)." These provisions attempt to prevent foreign firms from gaining unauthorized access to "critical technology, classified information, and special classes of classified information" through an acquisition of U.S. firms that it could not gain access through an export control license. This type of review is run independently of and parallel to a CFIUS review.

Critical Infrastructure/Key Resources

Arguably, the events of September 11, 2001, reshaped congressional attitudes toward the Exxon- Florio provision. This change in attitude became apparent in 2006 as a result of the public disclosure that Dubai Ports World[34] was attempting to purchase the British-owned P&O Ports,[35] with operations in various U.S. ports. After the September 11th terrorist attacks Congress passed and President Bush signed the USA PATRIOT Act of 2001 (Uniting and Strengthening America by Providing Appropriate Tools Required to Intercept and Obstruct Terrorism).[36] In this act, Congress provided for special support for "critical industries," which it defined as

> systems and assets, whether physical or virtual, so vital to the United States that the incapacity or destruction of such systems and assets would have a debilitating impact on security, national economic security, national public health or safety, or any combination of those matters.[37]

This broad definition is enhanced to some degree by other provisions of the act, which specifically identify sectors of the economy that Congress considers to be elements in the critical infrastructure of the nation. These sectors include telecommunications, energy, financial services, water, transportation sectors,[38] and the "cyber and physical infrastructure services critical to maintaining the national defense, continuity of government, economic prosperity, and quality of life in the United States."[39] The following year, Congress transferred the responsibility for identifying critical infrastructure to the Department of Homeland Security (DHS) through the Homeland Security Act of 2002.[40] In addition, the Homeland Security Act added key resources to the list of critical infrastructure (CI/KR) and defined those resources as: "publicly or privately controlled resources essential to the minimal operations of the economy and government."[41] Through a series of Directives, the Department of Homeland Security identified 17 sectors[42] of the economy as falling within the definition of critical infrastructure/key resources and assigned primary responsibility for those sectors to various Federal departments and agencies, which are designated as Sector-Specific Agencies (SSAs).[43] On March 3, 2008, Homeland Security Secretary Chertoff signed an internal DHS memo designating Critical Manufacturing as the 18th sector on the CI/KR list.

By adopting the terms "critical infrastructure" and "homeland security," following the events of September 11, 2001, Congress demonstrated that the attacks fundamentally altered the way many policymakers view the concept of national security. As a result, many policymakers have concluded that economic activities are a separately identifiable component of national security. In addition, many policymakers apparently perceive greater risks to the economy arising from foreign investments in which the foreign investor is owned or controlled by foreign governments as a result of the terrorist attacks. The Dubai Ports World case, in particular, demonstrated that there was a difference between the post-September 11 expectations held by many in Congress about the role of foreign investment in the economy and of economic infrastructure issues as a component of national security and the operations of CFIUS. For some Members of Congress, CFIUS seemed to be out of touch with the post-September 11, 2001, view of national security, because it remains founded in the late 1980s orientation of the Exxon-Florio provision, which views national security primarily in terms of national defense and downplays or even excludes a broader notion of economic national security.

Foreign Investment and National Security Act of 2007

In 2007, Congress changed the way foreign direct investments are reviewed through P.L. 110-49, the Foreign Investment and National Security Act of 2007.[44] Through P.L. 110-49, Congress strengthened its role in two fundamental ways. First, Congress enhanced its oversight capabilities by requiring greater reporting to Congress by CFIUS on the Committee's actions either during or after it completes reviews and investigations and by increasing reporting requirements on CFIUS. Second, Congress fundamentally altered the meaning of national security in the Exxon-Florio provision by including critical infrastructure and homeland security as areas of concern comparable to national security. The law also requires the Director of National Intelligence to conduct reviews of any investment that may pose a threat to the national security. The law provides for additional factors the President and CFIUS are required to use in assessing foreign investments, including the implications for the nation's critical infrastructure.

In another change, P.L. 110-49 requires CFIUS to investigate all foreign investment transactions in which the foreign entity is owned or controlled by a foreign government, regardless of the nature of the business. Some foreign investors may well regard this approach as a change in policy by the United States toward foreign investment. Prior to this change, foreign investment transactions were reviewed in a way that presumed that the transactions contributed positively to the economy. Consequently, the burden of proof was on the members of CFIUS to prove during a review that a particular transaction threatened to impair national security. P.L. 110-49, however, shifted the burden onto firms that are owned or controlled by a foreign government to prove that they are not a threat to national security. In any given year, the number of investment transactions in which the foreign investor is associated with a foreign government likely is small compared with the total number of foreign investment transactions. The number of such transactions, however, is growing as some foreign governments experience a surge in their foreign exchange reserves and they establish sovereign wealth funds in order to invest part of their reserve funds abroad in an array of activities, including in U.S. businesses. Many countries, such as China, also have state-owned enterprises that operate in the global economy.

To clarify U.S. policy toward foreign investment after the Dubai Ports World controversy and the impending passage of P.L. 110-49, President Bush released on May 10, 2007, a policy statement on open economies.[45] The statement offered strong support for the international flow of direct investment. In part, the statement reads:

> A free and open international investment regime is vital for a stable and growing economy, both here at home and throughout the world. The threat of global terrorism and other national security challenges have caused the United States and other countries to focus more intently on the national security dimensions of foreign investment. While my Administration will continue to take every necessary step to protect national security, my Administration recognizes that our prosperity and security are founded on our country's openness.
>
> As both the world's largest investor and the world's largest recipient of investment, the United States has a key stake in promoting an open investment regime. The United States unequivocally supports international investment in this country and is equally committed to securing fair, equitable, and nondiscriminatory treatment for U.S. investors abroad. Both inbound and outbound investment benefit our country by stimulating growth, creating jobs, enhancing productivity, and fostering competitiveness that allows our companies and their workers to prosper at home and in international markets. My Administration is committed to ensuring that the United States continues to be the most attractive place in the world to invest. I urge other nations to join us in supporting an open investment policy and protecting international investments.

The CFIUS process is just one of three major provisions of law that authorize the review of foreign direct investment transactions in the United States for their impact on the economy. The National Industrial Security Program and the critical industries provisions of various statutes also require that foreign direct investment transactions be reviewed. Generally, the reviews mandated by these three provisions operate independently, although at times they have overlapped. The provisions illustrate the complexities involved in defining most economic activities, which can span a broad range of economic activities and fields. Most economic activities affect various sectors and segments of the economy in ways that defy a narrow definition and complicate efforts to distinguish those economic activities that are related to the broad rubric of national security or to national economic security, which is even less clearly defined.

Strategic Materials Protection Board

The Strategic Materials Protection Board, created in 2006, could restrict other types of foreign investment transactions, although this likely will affect a small group of such transactions. In retrospect, some observers hope this provision will prevent future transactions similar to the 2005 merger between Magnequench International and the Canadian-owned firm AMR Technologies, Inc., which shifted ownership of the world's largest producer of Neo powder (composed of neodymium, iron, and boron) to produce Neo magnets.[46] The Strategic Materials Protection Board was mandated by Title VIII of the John Warner National Defense Authorization Act for Fiscal Year 2007, signed October 17, 2006, and designated as P.L. 109-364. The act established that the Strategic Materials Protection Board would be composed of representatives from: the Secretary of Defense; the Under Secretary of Defense for Acquisition, Technology, and Logistics; the Under Secretary of Defense for Intelligence; the Secretary of the Army; the Secretary of the Navy; and the Secretary of the Air Force. The Board is required to meet at least once every two years to make recommendations regarding materials critical to national security and to report to Congress on the results of meetings and on the recommendations of the Board. In addition, the act prohibits the Department of Defense from buying "strategic materials critical to national security" unless the metals are reprocessed, reused, or produced in the United States, except under a number of conditions, including the lack of availability of specialty metals.

The Board is directed in the statute to undertake four activities:

1. Determine the need to provide a long term domestic supply of materials designated as critical to national security to ensure that national defense needs are met.
2. Analyze the risk associated with each material designated as critical to national security and the effect on national defense that the non-availability of such material from a domestic source would have.
3. Recommend a strategy to the President to ensure the domestic availability of materials designated as critical to national security.
4. Recommend such other strategies to the President as the board considers appropriate to strengthen the industrial base with respect to materials critical to national security.

The Strategic Materials Protection Board met on July 17, 2007, and published a report in September 2007 of that meeting. At that meeting, the Board determined that the term "materials critical to national security" would mean "strategic materials critical to national security" as specified in the statute and would include those metals listed in Section 842 of P.L. 109-364 (10 U.S.C. 2533b). In this section, specialty metals are defined as:

1. Steel
   A) with a maximum alloy content exceeding one of more of the following limits" manganese, 1.65 percent, silicon, 0.60; or copper, 0.60 percent, or
   B) containing more than 0.25 percent of any of the following elements; aluminum, chromium, cobalt, columbium, molybdenum, nickel, titanium, tungsten, or vanadium.
2. Metal alloys consisting of nickel, iron-nickel, and cobalt base alloys containing a total of other alloying metals (except iron) in excess of 10 percent.
3. Titanium and titanium alloys.
4. Zirconium and zirconium base alloys.

Economic Considerations

The growing prominence of national security issues in the development of national foreign investment policies is raising questions about how policymakers can evaluate the economic costs and benefits of such measures when the measures are designed to restrict mergers, acquisitions, and take-overs of domestic firms by foreign investors for national security reasons. Indeed, such measures can sometimes focus more on achieving non-economic objectives than on achieving economic efficiency or on supporting a market-based allocation of resources. In addition, such policies often expose differing political and philosophical differences between policymakers within countries and among countries. Within the United States, for instance, such differences exist among Members of Congress and between Congress and the Administration over the role foreign investment should play in the economy. This analysis becomes especially complicated, because each nation has the authority to define its essential security concerns on its own terms and to adjust its foreign investment policy to meet that definition. As a result, such policies defy a straightforward cost-benefit analysis and can mask economic protectionism. This section discusses one possible framework for assessing the economic impact of more restrictive investment policies.

Part of the difficulty involved in assessing the economic impact is that at present there is no working set of parameters that establishes a functional definition of the national security implications of such economic activities as mergers, acquisitions, or take-overs of existing U.S. firms by foreign investors. This process of evaluation is even more difficult in peace time when there is no immediate national security threat posed by foreign investment that dictates the course of national security policies. In most cases, government actions to stop or curtail foreign direct investment in the form of a merger, an acquisition, or a take-over of an existing U.S., firm are mainly precautionary measures aimed at addressing potential future actions that a foreign investor may take.[47] This process of identification is also complicated on a multi-lateral basis, because each nation has its own definition of national security and its own approach to formulating policies regarding the role of economic activity within the national security rubric.

Whether intended or not, intervention in the economy on national security grounds creates a mix of industrial activities that most likely would not be achieved through traditional economic market forces. Such intervention often is associated with three types of economic activity. First, the intervention may involve efforts to prevent foreign firms from acquiring certain U.S. firms as a result of the type of economic activity that characterizes the U.S. firm or is related to the nature of the output produced by the U.S. firm. Second, opposition on national security grounds may arise as a result of concerns over the country of origin of the foreign acquirer. This type of concern has grown over the recent past because of the growing role of sovereign wealth funds controlled by foreign governments.

Third, national policies may provide special consideration for certain economic activities in the form of economic incentives for U.S. firms or barriers against foreign acquisition due to a belief that the targeted economic activities are important to national security. In some cases, intervention in the foreign investment process may be justified on a combination of economic and non- economic arguments. In these cases, the economic costs and benefits that accrue to the economy as a result of the policy actions may be tied directly to an assessment of the particular set of circumstances within which the cost-benefit analysis is conducted.

In the standard textbook presentation, economic production arises from a combination of the four main types of resources, or factors of production, namely: land, labor, capital, and entrepreneurial ability. Of these four factors, labor and capital are generally singled out due to their overwhelming importance in the production process. Growth within an economy, then, is generally believed to arise from growth in the two main factors of production, capital and labor, which are considered to be fixed at any particular point in time. Over time, however, the rate of growth in the labor force combined with the rate of growth in capital accumulation, or in the way in which capital is used, generally referred to as the rate of growth in productivity, set limits on the rate at which the economy can grow.

In a dynamic economy such as that of the United States, some sectors are expanding, or growing, at a rate that is faster than the economy as a whole, while other sectors are either declining, or are growing at a rate that is slower than the economy as a whole. Since the growth rate in the economy is governed by the rate of growth in the labor force and in productivity, any sector of the economy that grows faster than the average rate for the economy as a whole, can only do so by absorbing capital and labor from other sectors of the economy that, then, must be declining or growing at a rate that is less than the average for the economy as a whole, assuming that the economy is growing at close to full employment. Over time, the growing sectors of the economy necessarily take away capital and labor from the declining sectors of the economy. In the short- run, this transformative process may be uneven and may well lead to a mismatch in skills between sectors, which likely would result in some unused or underutilized resources.

Within the economy, economic theory maintains that demand and supply forces determine the market prices for labor and for capital as the various sectors compete for these scarce resources. These market prices, then, work to allocate resources within the economy among the vast array of economic activities into those activities that use the resources in the most efficient manner. Interference in this process, regardless of the reason, can cause a misallocation of resources in the economy and a loss of efficiency, which imposes a cost on the economy as a whole. In the case of government incentives, or subsidies, for a favored industry, the cost to the economy arises from two sources. The first is the direct cost involved in shifting resources into the protected sectors of the economy that are at variance with the way in which market forces would allocate those resources.

The second cost is the indirect cost that arises from the benefits that are lost to the economy from preventing resources, particularly foreign capital, from shifting into those sectors that would be gaining resources through market forces, or the opportunity cost to the economy that arises from a misallocation of resources. While mergers, acquisitions, or takeovers of existing U.S. firms by foreign investors imply at least a change in ownership, foreign investors may well possess additional technology, or other advantages that have made them successful international competitors that would be lost if such an investment were prevented for national security reasons. Economists argue that both direct and indirect costs arise when national policies are used to intervene in the foreign investment process, because such intervention generally is contrary to market forces which act to maximize production efficiencies.

Government policies that attempt to enhance national security by restricting acquisitions, mergers, and take-over of existing U.S. firms by foreign investors may also alter the allocation of capital within the economy and, thereby, incur short-term and long-term costs to the economy. For purposes of analysis, economists often divide production and other economic activities into two time periods: the short run and the long run. The distinction between the short run and the long run is not absolute, but is based on the ability of the economy to shift resources among sectors based on market forces. Generally, labor is thought to be the most mobile factor of production that can be shifted relatively quickly among sectors within the economy and at a lower short-run cost than capital. On the other hand, capital is generally thought of as comparatively more difficult to shift among economic sectors over the short-run. For instance, workers can shift into and out of jobs in response to market demand while it is difficult to shift production facilities or buildings from one locale to another. As a result, in the short run, labor is thought of as the variable factor of production, while capital is thought of as a fixed factor of production. In the long-run, however, all factors are viewed as variable since all of the factors can be reallocated to other sectors of the economy in response to shifts in long-term market forces. This division between the short run and the long run simply means that under normal market conditions, the costs of reallocating resources within the economy through public policy measures, or preventing the allocation of capital into certain sectors through foreign investment, that are not in tandem with market forces would accrue high short-run economic costs that would need an equally high combination of short-run and long-run benefits in order to justify the costs to the economy.

The distinction between the short-run and the long-run can change, depending on conditions within the economy that may require a shift in capital and labor among sectors of the economy. For instance, after the United States entered World War II, the U.S. economy shifted from a peace-time consumer-oriented economy to a war-time arms-producing economy within a relatively short period of time, because the external threats to the country were so great that a dramatic shift in the industrial mix of the economy was considered to be a necessary short-run cost that justified overriding market forces in order to produce quickly the material necessary to defend the nation. In this case, the benefits to the economy in terms of added security, principally the ability to defend the country from invasion or destruction, outweighed the short-run and long-run costs to the economy in terms of shifting resources into sectors of the economy that would not have been given priority under peace-time conditions.

In peace-time, without an imminent external threat, it is difficult to determine the economic parameters that define the terms "critical infrastructure," "homeland security," and "key resources." In addition, it is difficult to define clearly what role foreign investment should play as a separately definable component of national security. This is particularly true in the case of an individual economic transaction such as the acquisition of U.S. firm by a foreign firm. In these cases, the threats to the country often are not well defined or understood and it often is not an easy proposition to evaluate the costs and benefits to the economy as a whole of protecting or promoting certain economic activities. Similarly, it is often difficult to determine the national security elements of allowing or barring investors who are of certain foreign nationalities from acquiring U.S. firms. This problem is compounded under the current "War on Terrorism" in which potential threats to the United States may be decentralized and originate in sub-national organizations.

When policymakers decide to promote certain types of economic activities or to protect U.S. firms or economic activities from foreign investment on the grounds of national security, those officials are in effect weighing the costs and benefits to the nation, or more specifically the marginal costs and marginal benefits, of intervening to alter the mix of industrial activity in the economy. The costs in this case would include the direct short-run and long-run marginal costs associated with blocking foreign capital from being invested in certain favored sectors of the economy in contravention of market forces and, in the case of incentives for favored industries, the indirect costs involved in reducing the available capital and labor that could be used in the economy for more productive activities, or the opportunity cost of the labor and capital.

The marginal benefits that accrue to the nation from such policy activities arise from a combination of a number of factors. The nation may well benefit from the perceived gain in national security and the economy may gain through the capital inflow that is represented by the foreign investment in the form of a merger, acquisition, or take-over of an existing U.S. firm. Foreign investors may also benefit the economy by bringing technological or other production advantages to the United States. Foreign investment may also benefit the economy by sustaining jobs and by producing actual goods and services. These benefits may also include what may be termed the "national security" component of production, or that part of production that satisfies national security concerns. Presumably, the economic benefits would need to be at least as great as the non-economic benefits in order for national policymakers to justify the economic costs. If non-economic benefits comprise the largest share of the expected benefits that arise from the policy action, such a policy course might be economic protectionism in the guise of national security and policymakers may realize greater benefits for the nation by pursuing a different policy course that accrues fewer economic costs.

In addition, the economic and non-economic benefits that are associated with a particular policy may accrue to a large contingent within the economy, as would be the case in a national emergency, or they may accrue to a few as is often the case with economic protectionism. While this distinction between the dispersion of beneficiaries and the allocation of the benefits within the economy is not an absolute way of evaluating national investment policies, it does provide one measure for assessing the distinction between measures that accrue high economic costs relative to few economic benefits within the economy as a whole and may argue in favor of pursuing a different policy course. In some cases the citizens of a nation may be willing to absorb high short-run and long-run costs in order to achieve some non-economic national security goal that benefits a small contingent within the economy. In such a case, however, it may be possible to achieve such a national security goal through means other than through foreign investment policies that entail lower costs for the economy.

The national security component of production may also be equated with a non-economic good that satisfies a national or social objective related to some public assessment of national security. The basis for such non-economic national security benefits can be thought of as a spectrum of benefits that are associated with a similar spectrum of national security threats. These threats can then be thought of as running from threats of imminent destruction that would affect the economy as a whole to concerns about potential activities that are at best tangentially associated with national security and that affect a narrow set of workers and a limited amount of capital. As a result of this spectrum of potential versus real threats and the dangers the threats pose to the economy, the benefits associated with policies that are advanced on the grounds of national security will be stronger or weaker depending on the context within which the argument is made.

Regardless of the nature of the national security threat, the direct and indirect costs to the economy that arise from intervention in the investment process may be the same and pose costs to the economy. Since the costs to the economy that arise from intervention likely are the same, the key to public policy choices is the perceived benefits that are associated with satisfying or addressing such national security concerns. In this way, the marginal costs associated with intervention are equivalent to the marginal benefits that are derived from the policy actions and may be thought of as the cost of satisfying such national security concerns. In the time of full- scale war, the costs to the country of intervening in the economy to redirect resources to produce defense and war material are justified on the basis of the obvious benefits that arise from national survival. In less dire circumstances, however, such cost-benefit comparisons are a great deal more difficult to make.

CONCLUSION

Following the terrorist attacks of September 11, 2001, policymakers in the United States and abroad have increased their scrutiny of foreign investment in their economies as a component of national security. There is no precise way, however, to estimate the exact dollar amount for the economic costs and benefits of national policies that attempt to direct or restrict foreign direct investment for national security concerns. Also, it can be difficult to determine if foreign investment policies ultimately result in enhanced national security or are a form of economic protectionism. In concept, the economic costs and benefits associated with restrictive foreign investment policies can be evaluated to determine the overall impact of such policies on the long- run economic performance of country. Evaluating and assessing the national security importance of such policies is complicated, however, because any such assessment naturally occurs within the context with which the assessment takes place. A nation facing an imminent threat of destruction or annihilation is willing to accept extraordinarily high economic costs in order to address such a danger

Within the United States, the proposed acquisition of P&O Ports by Dubai Ports World in 2006 and the growing presence of investors that are owned or controlled by foreign governments has sparked a debate between Members of Congress and the Administration over the role of foreign investment in the economy. Part of this debate is focused on determining a working set of parameters that establish a functional definition of the national security implications of foreign direct investment. In part, this issue reflects differing assessments of the economic impact of foreign investment on the economy and differing political and philosophical views among Members of Congress and between the Congress and the Administration.

Since 2006, the United States has participated in discussions spearheaded by the OECD to develop a set of best practices to serve as guidelines for national policies that restrict foreign investment for national security objectives. Presently, the participants have agreed that each nation is its own best judge of its national security interests. At the same time, they have agreed that national policies that restrict foreign investment for national security reasons should be transparent, predictable, and non-discriminatory. The final OECD report is scheduled for release in May 2009 and likely will contain a set of best practices that Members of Congress may opt to review as a guide concerning U.S. laws and regulations that govern the U.S. treatment of foreign investment relative to U.S. national security objectives.

There are a number of factors that complicate efforts to assess the impact of policies that restrict foreign investment for national security concerns. Some of those factors include the difficulties that are involved in attaching a precise dollar amount to the economic costs and benefits that are associated with such foreign investment policies. One possible framework for assessing such policies is based on the concept of marginal costs and benefits to the nation that accrue from policies that restrict foreign investment. In this case the benefits are some combination of the economic and non-economic benefits that might be expected to arise from the restrictions, while the costs include a set of real costs that the economy would be expected to incur as a result of the policies. Measures that restrict foreign direct investment that are based on expectations of achieving large non-economic benefits relative to economic benefits and to large economic costs may not be an effective tool. Instead, there may be other policy tools that could utilized to achieve the same goal, but with lower costs to the economy.

While not determinative, another way of assessing such restrictions is by examining the dispersion of the benefits throughout the economy. At times a nation may well be willing to absorb the high costs that could be involved in protecting some economic activities by restricting or controlling foreign investment. Generally, though it seems reasonable to assume that a policy that is implemented in order to restrict foreign investment that offers benefits to a small group of individuals within the economy and that entails high economic costs relative to benefits, especially where non-economic benefits are a large share of the expected benefits, could be replaced by other measures that accrue lower costs to the economy.

End Notes

[1] CRS Report RL33103, *Foreign Investment in the United States: Major Federal Statutory Restrictions*, by Michael V. Seitzinger.

[2] P.L. 110-49 originated in the first session of the 110th Congress as S. 1610, the Foreign Investment and National Security Act of 2007, introduced by Senator Dodd on June 13, 2007. On June 29, 2007, the Senate adopted S. 1610 in lieu of a competing House version, H.R. 556 by unanimous consent. On July 11, 2007, the House accepted the Senate's version of H.R. 556 by a vote of 370-45 and sent the measure to the President, who signed it on July 26, 2007. On January 23, 2008, President Bush issued Executive Order 13456 implementing the law.

[3] Scott, Sarah P., U.S. International Transactions: First Quarter of 2012. *Survey of Current Business*, July 2012, p. 59. Direct investment data reported in the balance of payments differ from capital flow data reported elsewhere, because the balance of payments data have not been adjusted for current cost adjustments to earnings.

[4] The position, or stock, is the net book value of foreign direct investors' equity in, and outstanding loans to, their affiliates in the United States. A change in the position in a given year consists of three components: equity and intercompany inflows, reinvested earnings of incorporated affiliates, and valuation adjustments to account for changes in the value of financial assets. The Department of Commerce also publishes data on the foreign direct investment position valued on a current-cost and market value bases. These estimates indicate that in 2011 foreign direct investment increased by $311 billion measured at current cost to a cumulative value of $2.9 trillion, while the market value measure rose by $112 billion in to reach a cumulative value of $3.5 trillion.

[5] Barefoot, Kevin B., and Marilyn Ibarra-Caton, Direct Investment Positions for 2011: Country and Industry Detail, *Survey of Current Business*, July 2012. p. 20.

[6] The United States defines direct investment abroad as the ownership or control, directly or indirectly, by one person (individual, branch, partnership, association, government, etc.) of

10% or more of the voting securities of an incorporated business enterprise or an equivalent interest in an unincorporated business enterprise. 15 CFR § 806.15 (a)(1).

[7] Thomas, Sarah Scott, Erin M. Whitaker, U.S. International Transactions: Second Quarter of 2010. *Survey of Current Business*, October 2010, p. 62. Direct investment data reported in the balance of payments differ from capital flow data reported elsewhere, because the balance of payments data have not been adjusted for current cost adjustments to earnings.

[8] *World Investment Report 2012*, United Nations, July 2012, p. 1.

[9] For additional information, see CRS Report RL34336, *Sovereign Wealth Funds: Background and Policy Issues for Congress*, by Martin A. Weiss.

[10] *World Investment Report, 2007*, p. 14.

[11] For additional information, see CRS Report RS21128, *The Organization for Economic Cooperation and Development*, by James K. Jackson.

[12] *International Investment Perspectives: Freedom of Investment in a Changing World, 207 Edition*, Organization for Economic Cooperation and Development, 2007, p. 105.

[13] Ibid., p. 100.

[14] Friedman, Benjamin H., The Terrible 'Ifs', *Regulation,* Winter 2007/2008, pp. 32-40.

[15] Enders, Walter and Todd Sandler, Terrorism and Foreign Direct Investment in Spain and Greece, in Sandler, Todd, and Keith Hartley, eds., *The Economics of Conflict*, Vol. II. Cheltenham, UK; Northhamption, MA; Edward Elgar, 2003.

[16] *Freedom of Investment, National Security and "Strategic" Industries: Progress Report by the OECD Investment Committee*. Organization for Economic Cooperation and Development, April 2008; *Eighth Roundtable on Freedom of Investment, National Security and "Strategic" Industries*, OECD, October 8, 2008.

[17] *International Investment Perspectives*, p. 55.

[18] The members of the project include the 30 members of the OECD, the 10 non-member adherents to the Declaration (Argentina, Brazil, Chile, Egypt, Estonia, Israel, Latvia, Lithuania, Romania, and Slovenia), Russia, and other countries that attended at least one session: China, India, Indonesia, and South Africa.

[19] *Transparency and Predictability for Investment Policies Addressing National Security Concerns: A Survey of Practices.* Organization for Economic Cooperation and Development, May 2008.

[20] *Proportionality of Security-Related Investment Instruments: A Survey of Practices*. Organization for Economic Cooperation and Development, May 2008.

[21] The Group of Eight nations includes Canada, France, Germany, Italy, Japan, Russia, the United Kingdom, and the United States.

[22] *Growth and Responsibility in the World Economy*, G8 Summit Declaration, June 7, 2007. Paragraphs 10 and 11.

[23] *Fourth Report on G-20 Investment Measures*, Organization for Economic Cooperation and Development, November 2010.

[24] *Protection of "Critical Infrastructure" and the Role of Investment Policies Relating to National Security,* The Organization for Economic Cooperation and Development, May 2008, p. 2.

[25] *Protection of Critical Infrastructure and the Role of Investment Policies Relating to National Security*, p. 6.

[26] Ibid., p. 8.

[27] Such linkages appear to be important factors for both developed and developing host countries, see Alfaro, Laura, Areendum Chanda, Sebnem Kalemli-Ozcam, and Selin Sayek, *How Does Foreign Direct Investment Promote Economic Growth? Exploring the Effects of Financial Markets on Linkages.* Working Paper 12522, September 2006, National Bureau of Economic Research.

[28] Seitzinger, *Foreign Investment in the United States: Major Federal Restrictions*.

[29] For additional information, see CRS Report RL33312, *The Exon-Florio National Security Test for Foreign Investment*, by James K. Jackson.

[30] P.L. 100-418, title V, Subtitle A, Part II, or 50 U.S.C. app 2170.

[31] For additional information, see CRS Report RL33388, *The Committee on Foreign Investment in the United States (CFIUS)*, by James K. Jackson.

[32] Ibid.

[33] Senate Armed Services Committee, Briefing on the Dubai Ports World Ports Deal, February 23, 2006.

[34] Dubai Ports World was created in November 2005 by integrating Dubai Ports Authority and Dubai Ports International. It is one of the largest commercial port operators in the world with operations in the Middle East, India, Europe, Asia, Latin America, the Caribbean, and North America.

[35] Peninsular and Oriental Steam Company is a leading ports operator and transport company with operations in ports, ferries, and property development. It operates container terminals and logistics operations in over 100 ports and has a presence in 18 countries.

[36] P.L. 107-56, title X, Sec. 1014, October 26, 2001; 42 U.S.C. Sec. 5195c(e).

[37] Ibid.

[38] 42 U.S.C. Sec. 5195c(b)(2).

[39] 42 U.S.C. Sec. 5195c(b)(3).

[40] P.L. 107-296, Sec. 2, November 25, 2002; 6 U.S.C. Sec. 101.

[41] 6 U.S.C. Sec. 101(9).

[42] The original sectors include 1) Agriculture and Food; 2) Defense Industrial Base; 3) Energy; 4) Public Health and Healthcare; 5) National Monuments and Icons; 6) Banking and Finance; 7) Drinking Water and Water Treatment Systems; 8) Chemical; 9) Commercial Facilities; 10) Dams; 11) Emergency Services; 12) Commercial Nuclear Reactors, Materials, and Waste; 13) Information Technology; 14) Telecommunications; 15) Postal and Shipping; 16) Transportation Systems; and 17) Government Facilities.

[43] Sector-Specific Agencies include the Departments of: Agriculture, Defense, Energy, Health and Human Services, Homeland Security, Interior, Treasury, and the Environmental Protection Agency.

[44] P.L. 110-49 originated in the first session of the 110th Congress as S. 1610, the Foreign Investment and National Security Act of 2007, introduced by Senator Dodd on June 13, 2007. On June 29, 2007, the Senate adopted S. 1610 in lieu of a competing House version, H.R. 556, by unanimous consent. On July 11, 2007, the House accepted the Senate's version of H.R. 556 by a vote of 370-45 and sent the measure to the President, who signed it on July 26, 2007. On January 23, 2008, President Bush issued Executive Order 13456 implementing the law.

[45] President Bush's statement is available at http://georgewbush-whitehouse.archives.gov/news/releases/2007/05/ 20070510-2.html.

[46] Neo magnets have a broad range of uses in products where strong magnetic properties are required in conjunction with small size and weight, including hard disk drives, optical disk drives, printers, faxes, scanners, camcorders, game consoles, pagers, PDA's, mobile phones, mp3 players, video recorders, transmission speed sensors in automobiles, airbag sensors, instrument gauges, bearings, generators, cordless power tools, refrigerators, air conditioners, and such military applications as magnets in the motors of the U.S. Joint Direct Attack Munition, or smart bombs.

[47] *International Investment Perspectives*, p. 54-63.

In: Foreign Investment in the U.S.
Editor: Theodore L. Newell

ISBN: 978-1-62948-930-8

Chapter 5

THE COMMITTEE ON FOREIGN INVESTMENT IN THE UNITED STATES (CFIUS)*

James K. Jackson

SUMMARY

The Committee on Foreign Investment in the United States (CFIUS) is comprised of nine members, two ex officio members, and other members as appointed by the President representing major departments and agencies within the federal executive branch. While the group generally has operated in relative obscurity, the proposed acquisition of commercial operations at six U.S. ports by Dubai Ports World in 2006 placed the group's operations under intense scrutiny by Members of Congress and the public. Prompted by this case, some Members of the 109th and 110th Congresses questioned the ability of Congress to exercise its oversight responsibilities given the general view that CFIUS's operations lack transparency. Other Members revisited concerns about the linkage between national security and the role of foreign investment in the U.S. economy. Some Members of Congress and others argued that the nation's security and economic concerns have changed since the September 11, 2001, terrorist attacks and that these concerns were not being reflected

* This is an edited, reformatted and augmented version of the Congressional Research Service Publication, CRS Report for Congress RL33388, dated June 12, 2013.

sufficiently in the Committee's deliberations. In addition, anecdotal evidence seemed to indicate that the CFIUS process was not market neutral. Instead, a CFIUS investigation of an investment transaction may have been perceived by some firms and by some in the financial markets as a negative factor that added to uncertainty and may have spurred firms to engage in behavior that may not have been optimal for the economy as a whole. In the 112th Congress, some Members expressed their concerns to the Obama Administration over the national security implications of a proposed acquisition of a U.S. technology company by the Chinese-owned Huawei Technologies.

In the first session of the 110th Congress, the House and Senate adopted S. 1610, the Foreign Investment and National Security Act (FINSA) of 2007. On July 11, 2007, the measure was sent to President Bush, who signed it on July 26, 2007. It is designated as P.L. 110-49. On January 23, 2008, President Bush issued Executive Order 13456 implementing the law. The Executive Order also established some caveats that may affect the way in which the law is implemented. These caveats stipulate that the President will provide information that is required under the law as long as it is "consistent" with the President's authority "to (i) conduct the foreign affairs of the United States; (ii) withhold information the disclosure of which could impair the foreign relations, the national security, the deliberative processes of the Executive, or the performance of the Executive's constitutional duties; (iii) recommend for congressional consideration such measures as the President may judge necessary and expedient; and (iv) supervise the unitary executive branch." Despite the relatively recent passage of the amendments, some Members of Congress and others have questioned the performance of CFIUS and the way the Committee reviews cases involving foreign governments, particularly with the emergence of direct investments through sovereign wealth funds (SWFs). The Obama Administration issued a statement on June 30, 2011, supporting an open investment policy, a commitment to treat all investors in a fair and equitable manner, and support for business investment from sources both home and abroad in the economy. On September 28, 2012, President Obama used the authority granted to him under FINSA to block a Chinese acquisition of a U.S. energy firm.

BACKGROUND

The Committee on Foreign Investment in the United States (CFIUS) is an interagency committee that serves the President in overseeing the national security implications of foreign investment in the economy. Originally established by an Executive Order of President Ford in 1975, the committee generally has operated in relative obscurity.[1] According to a Treasury Department memorandum, the Committee originally was established in order to placate Congress, which had grown concerned over the rapid increase in investments by Organization of the Petroleum Exporting Countries (OPEC) countries in American portfolio assets (Treasury securities, corporate stocks and bonds), and to respond to concerns of some that much of the OPEC investments were being driven by political, rather than by economic, motives.[2]

Thirty years later, public and congressional concerns about the proposed purchase of commercial port operations of the British-owned Peninsular and Oriental Steam Navigation Company (P&O)[3] in six U.S. ports by Dubai Ports World (DP World)[4] sparked a firestorm of criticism and congressional activity during the 109th Congress concerning CFIUS and the manner in which it operates. Some Members of Congress and the public argued that the nation's economic and national security concerns had fundamentally changed as a result of the September 11, 2001, terrorist attacks on the United States and that these changes required a reassessment of the role of foreign investment in the economy and in the nation's security. As a result of the attention by both the public and Congress, DP World officials announced that they would sell off the U.S. port operations to an American owner.[5] On December 11, 2006, DP World officials announced that a unit of AIG Global Investment Group, a New York-based asset management company with large assets, but no experience in port operations, would acquire the U.S. port operations for an undisclosed amount.[6]

Members of Congress introduced more than 25 bills in the second session of the 109th Congress that addressed various aspects of foreign investment since the proposed DP World transaction. In the first session of the 110th Congress, Members approved, and President Bush signed, a measure that was designated as P.L. 110-49 that alters the CFIUS process in order to provide greater oversight by Congress and increased reporting by the Committee on its decisions. In addition, P.L. 110-49 broadened the definition of national security and required greater scrutiny by CFIUS of certain types of foreign direct investments. The law demonstrated the concern some Members had with the way CFIUS operated and with the lack of transparency in the CFIUS review process that some Members believed had hampered Congress's ability to exercise its oversight responsibilities. Not all Members were satisfied with the law. Some Members argued that the law remained deficient in reviewing investment by foreign governments through sovereign wealth funds (SWFs), an issue that was just beginning to attract attention when the law was adopted. In early 2011, some Members of Congress had requested that the Obama Administration support a recommendation by CFIUS that the President block a proposed acquisition of 3Leaf Systems by Huawei Technologies over national security concerns. Instead, Huawei discontinued its efforts to acquire the U.S. firm.

ESTABLISHMENT OF CFIUS

President Ford's 1975 Executive Order established the basic structure of CFIUS, and directed that the "representative"[7] of the Secretary of the Treasury be the chairman of the Committee. The Executive Order also stipulated that the Committee would have "the primary continuing responsibility within the executive branch for monitoring the impact of foreign investment in the United States, both direct and portfolio, and for coordinating the implementation of United States policy on such investment." In particular, CFIUS was directed to (1) arrange for the preparation of analyses of trends and significant developments in foreign investments in the United States; (2) provide guidance on arrangements with foreign governments for advance consultations on prospective major foreign governmental investments in the United States; (3) review investments in the United States which, in the judgment of the Committee, might have major implications for United States national interests; and (4) consider proposals for new legislation or regulations relating to foreign investment as may appear necessary.[8]

President Ford's Executive Order also stipulated that information submitted "in confidence shall not be publicly disclosed" and that information submitted to CFIUS be used "only for the purpose of carrying out the functions and activities" of the order. In addition, the Secretary of Commerce was directed to perform a number of activities, including

(1) obtaining, consolidating, and analyzing information on foreign investment in the United States;
(2) improving the procedures for the collection and dissemination of information on such foreign investment;
(3) the close observing of foreign investment in the United States;
(4) preparing reports and analyses of trends and of significant developments in appropriate categories of such investment;

(5) compiling data and preparing evaluation of significant transactions; and
(6) submitting to the Committee on Foreign Investment in the United States appropriate reports, analyses, data, and recommendations as to how information on foreign investment can be kept current.

The Executive Order, however, raised questions among various observers and government officials who doubted that federal agencies had the legal authority to collect the types of data that were required by the order. As a result, Congress and the President sought to clarify this issue, and in the following year President Ford signed the International Investment Survey Act of 1976.[9] The act gave the President "clear and unambiguous authority" to collect information on "international investment." In addition, the act authorized "the collection and use of information on direct investments owned or controlled directly or indirectly by foreign governments or persons, and to provide analyses of such information to the Congress, the executive agencies, and the general public."[10]

By 1980, some Members of Congress had come to believe that CFIUS was not fulfilling its mandate. Between 1975 and 1980, for instance, the Committee had met only 10 times and seemed unable to decide whether it should respond to the political or the economic aspects of foreign direct investment in the United States.[11] One critic of the Committee argued in a congressional hearing in 1979 that, "the Committee has been reduced over the last four years to a body that only responds to the political aspects or the political questions that foreign investment in the United States poses and not with what we really want to know about foreign investments in the United States, that is: Is it good for the economy?"[12]

From 1980 to 1987, CFIUS investigated a number of foreign investments, mostly at the request of the Department of Defense. In 1983, for instance, a Japanese firm sought to acquire a U.S. specialty steel producer. The Department of Defense subsequently classified the metals produced by the firm because they were used in the production of military aircraft, which caused the Japanese firm to withdraw its offer. Another Japanese company attempted to acquire a U.S. firm in 1985 that manufactured specialized ball bearings for the military. The acquisition was completed after the Japanese firm agreed that production would be maintained in the United States. In a similar case in 1987, the Defense Department objected to a proposed acquisition of the computer division of a U.S. multinational company by a French firm because of classified work engaged in by the computer division.

The acquisition proceeded after the classified contracts were reassigned to the U.S. parent company.[13]

The "Exon-Florio" Provision

In 1988, amid concerns over foreign acquisition of certain types of U.S. firms, particularly by Japanese firms, Congress approved the Exon-Florio provision.[14] This statute grants the President the authority to block proposed or pending foreign "mergers, acquisitions, or takeovers" of "persons engaged in interstate commerce in the United States" that threaten to impair the national security. Congress directed, however, that before this authority can be invoked the President must conclude that other U.S. laws are inadequate or inappropriate to protect the national security, and that he must have "credible evidence" that the foreign investment will impair the national security. This same standard was maintained in P.L. 110-49.

By the late 1980s, Congress and the public had grown increasingly concerned about the sharp increase in foreign investment in the United States and the potential impact such investment might have on the U.S. economy. In particular, the proposed sale in 1987 of Fairchild Semiconductor Co. by Schlumberger Ltd. of France to Fujitsu Ltd. of Japan touched off strong opposition in Congress and provided much of the impetus behind the passage of the Exon-Florio provision. The proposed Fairchild acquisition generated intense concern in Congress in part because of general difficulties in trade relations with Japan at that time and because some Americans felt that the United States was declining as an international economic power as well as a world power. The Defense Department opposed the acquisition because some officials believed that the deal would give Japan control over a major supplier of computer chips for the military and would make U.S. defense industries more dependent on foreign suppliers for sophisticated high-technology products.[15]

Although Commerce Secretary Malcolm Baldridge and Defense Secretary Caspar Weinberger failed in their attempt to have President Reagan block the Fujitsu acquisition, Fujitsu and Schlumberger called off the proposed sale of Fairchild.[16] While Fairchild was acquired some months later by National Semiconductor Corp. for a discount,[17] the Fujitsu-Fairchild incident marked an important shift in the Reagan Administration's support for unlimited foreign direct investment in U.S. businesses and boosted support within the

Administration for fixed guidelines for blocking foreign takeovers of companies in national security-sensitive industries.[18]

In 1988, after three years of often contentious negotiations between Congress and the Reagan Administration, Congress passed and President Reagan signed the Omnibus Trade and Competitiveness Act of 1988.[19] The Exon-Florio provision, which was included as Section 5021 of that act, fundamentally transformed CFIUS. The provision originated in bills reported by the Commerce Committee in the Senate and the Energy and Commerce Committee in the House, but the measure was transferred to the Senate Banking Committee as a result of a dispute over jurisdictional responsibilities.[20] In 1990, President Bush, using the authority granted under the Exon-Florio provision, directed the China National Aero-Technology Import and Export Corporation (CATIC) to divest its acquisition of MAMCO Manufacturing, a Seattle-based firm producing metal parts and assemblies for aircraft, because of concerns that CATIC might gain access to technology through Mamco that it would otherwise have to obtain under an export license.[21]

Part of Congress's motivation in adopting the Exon-Florio provision apparently arose from concerns that foreign takeovers of U.S. firms could not be stopped unless the President declared a national emergency or regulators invoked federal antitrust, environmental, or securities laws. Through the Exon-Florio provision, Congress attempted to strengthen the President's hand in conducting foreign investment policy, while limiting its own role as a means of emphasizing that, as much as possible, the commercial nature of investment transactions should be free from political considerations. Congress also attempted to balance public concerns about the economic impact of certain types of foreign investment with the nation's long-standing international commitment to maintaining an open and receptive environment for foreign investment.

Furthermore, Congress did not intend to have the Exon-Florio provision alter the generally open foreign investment climate of the country or to have it inhibit foreign direct investments in industries that could not be considered to be of national security interest. At the time, some analysts believed the provision could potentially widen the scope of industries that fell under the national security rubric. CFIUS, however, is not free to establish an independent approach to reviewing foreign investment transactions, but operates under the authority of the President and reflects his attitudes and policies. As a result, the discretion CFIUS uses to review and to investigate foreign investment cases reflects policy guidance from the President. Foreign investors also are constrained by legislation that bars foreign direct investment in such industries as maritime, aircraft, banking, resources, and power.[22] Generally, these sectors were closed to foreign investors prior to passage of the Exon-Florio provision in order to prevent public services and public interest activities from falling under foreign control, primarily for national defense purposes.

Through Executive Order 12661, President Reagan implemented provisions of the Omnibus Trade Act. In the Executive Order, President Reagan delegated his authority to administer the Exon-Florio provision to CFIUS,[23] particularly to conduct reviews, to undertake investigations, and to make recommendations, although the statute itself does not specifically mention CFIUS. As a result of President Reagan's action, CFIUS was transformed from a purely administrative body with limited authority to review and analyze data on foreign investment to one with a broad mandate and significant authority to advise the President on foreign investment transactions and to recommend that some transactions be blocked.

TREASURY DEPARTMENT REGULATIONS

After extensive public comment, the Treasury Department issued its final regulations in November 1991 implementing the Exon-Florio provision.[24] Although these procedures were amended through P.L. 110-49, they continued to serve as the basis for the Exon-Florio review and investigation until new regulations were released on November 21, 2008.[25] These regulations created an essentially voluntary system of notification by the parties to an acquisition and they allowed for notices of acquisitions by agencies that are members of CFIUS. Despite the voluntary nature of the notification, firms largely comply with the provision, because the regulations stipulate that foreign acquisitions that are governed by the Exon-Florio review process that do not notify the Committee remain subject indefinitely to divestment or other appropriate actions by the President. Under most circumstances, notice of a proposed acquisition that is given to the Committee by a third party, including shareholders, is not considered by the Committee to constitute an official notification. The regulations also indicated that notifications provided to the Committee would be considered to be confidential and the information would not be released by the Committee to the press or commented on publicly.

The "Byrd Amendment"

In 1992, Congress amended the Exon-Florio statute through Section 837(a) of the National Defense Authorization Act for Fiscal Year 1993 (P.L. 102-484). Known as the "Byrd" amendment after the amendment's sponsor, the provision requires CFIUS to investigate proposed mergers, acquisitions, or takeovers in cases where two criteria are met:

(1) the acquirer is controlled by or acting on behalf of a foreign government; and
(2) the acquisition results in control of a person engaged in interstate commerce in the United States that could affect the national security of the United States.[26]

This amendment came under intense scrutiny by the 109th Congress as a result of the DP World transaction. Many Members of Congress and others believed that this amendment required CFIUS to undertake a full 45-day investigation of the transaction because DP World was "controlled by or acting on behalf of a foreign government." The DP World acquisition, however, exposed a sharp rift between what some Members apparently believed the amendment directed CFIUS to do and how the members of CFIUS were interpreting the amendment. In particular, some Members of Congress apparently interpreted the amendment to direct CFIUS to conduct a mandatory 45-day investigation if the foreign firm involved in a transaction is owned or controlled by a foreign government. Representatives of CFIUS argued that they interpreted the amendment to mean that a 45-day investigation was discretionary and not mandatory. In the case of the DP World acquisition, CFIUS representatives argued that they had concluded as a result of an extensive review of the proposed acquisition prior to the case being formally filed with CFIUS and during the 30-day review that the DP World case did not warrant a full 45-day investigation. They conceded that the case met the first criterion under the Byrd amendment, because DP World was controlled by a foreign government, but that it did not meet the second part of the requirement, because CFIUS had concluded during the 30-day review that the transaction "could not affect the national security."[27]

The intense public and congressional reaction that arose from the proposed Dubai Ports World acquisition spurred the Bush Administration in late 2006 to make an important administrative change in the way CFIUS reviewed foreign investment transactions. CFIUS and President Bush approved the acquisition of Lucent Technologies, Inc. by the French-based Alcatel SA, which was completed on December 1, 2006. Before the transaction was approved by CFIUS, however, Alcatel-Lucent was required to agree to a national security arrangement, known as a Special Security Arrangement, or SSA, that restricts Alcatel's access to sensitive work done by Lucent's research arm, Bell Labs, and the communications infrastructure in the United States.

The most controversial feature of this arrangement is that it allows CFIUS to reopen a review of the deal and to overturn its approval at any time if CFIUS believed the companies "materially fail to comply" with the terms of the arrangement. This marks a significant changed in the CFIUS process. Prior to this transaction, CFIUS reviews and investigations had been portrayed, and had been considered, to be final. As a result, firms were willing to subject themselves voluntarily to a CFIUS review, because they believed that once an investment transaction was scrutinized and approved by the members of CFIUS the firms could be assured that the investment transaction would be exempt from any future reviews or actions. This administrative change, however, meant that a CFIUS determination may no longer be a final decision and it added a new level of uncertainty to foreign investors seeking to acquire U.S. firms. A broad range of U.S. and international business groups objected to this change in the Bush Administration's policy.[28]

THE AMENDED CFIUS PROCESS

In the first session of the 110th Congress, Representative Maloney introduced H.R. 556, the National Security Foreign Investment Reform and Strengthened Transparency Act of 2007, on January 18, 2007. The measure was approved by the House Financial Services Committee on February 13, 2007, with amendments, and was approved with additional amendments by the full House on February 28, 2007, by a vote of 423 to 0. On June 13, 2007, Senator Dodd introduced S. 1610, the Foreign Investment and National Security Act of 2007. On June 29, 2007, the Senate adopted S. 1610 in lieu of H.R. 556 by unanimous consent. On July 11, 2007, the House accepted the Senate's version of H.R. 556 by a vote of 370-45 and sent the measure to the President, who signed it on July 26, 2007. It is designated as P.L. 110-49. On January 23, 2008, President Bush issued Executive Order 13456 implementing the law. The Executive Order makes a number of substantive changes to the law. This report incorporates the changes made by this statute and by the Executive Order.

P.L. 110-49 establishes CFIUS by statutory authority and has the Secretary of the Treasury serve as the Chairman of CFIUS. The measure follows the same pattern that was set by Executive Order by allotting the Committee 30 days to conduct a review, 45 days to conduct an investigation, and 15 days for the President to make his determination. The President retains his authority as the only officer with the authority to suspend or prohibit mergers, acquisitions, and takeovers, and the measure places additional requirements on firms that resubmitted a filing after previously withdrawing a filing before a full review is completed.

Over time, the three step Exon-Florio process apparently had evolved to include an informal stage of unspecified length of time that consists of an unofficial CFIUS determination prior to the formal filing with CFIUS. This type of informal review had developed because it likely served the interests of both CFIUS and the firms that were involved in an investment transaction. According to Treasury Department officials, this informal contact enabled "CFIUS staff to identify potential issues before the review process formally begins."[29] This informal process has continued under the provisions of P.L. 110-49.

Firms that are party to an investment transaction apparently have benefitted from this informal review in a number of ways. For one, it allowed firms additional time to work out any national security concerns privately with individual CFIUS members. Secondly, and perhaps more importantly, it provided a process for firms to avoid risking potential negative publicity that could arise if a transaction were to be blocked or otherwise labeled as impairing U.S. national security interests. For some firms, public knowledge of a CFIUS investigation has had a negative effect on the value of the firm's stock price.

For CFIUS members, the informal process has been beneficial because it has given them as much time as they have felt was necessary to review a transaction without facing the time constraints that arise under the formal CFIUS review process. This informal review likely has also given the CFIUS members added time to negotiate with the firms involved in a transaction to restructure the transaction in ways that have addressed any potential security concerns or to develop other types of conditions that members feel are appropriate in order to remove security concerns.

On January 23, 2008, President Bush issued Executive Order 13456, which implemented P.L. 110-49 and made various changes to the law. The

Committee consists of nine members, including the Secretaries of State, the Treasury, Defense, Homeland Security, Commerce, and Energy; the Attorney General; the United States Trade Representative; and the Director of the Office of Science and Technology Policy.[30] The Secretary of Labor and the Director of National Intelligence serve as ex officio members of the Committee.[31] The Executive Order 13456 also added five more members to CFIUS in order to "observe and, as appropriate, participate in and report to the President:" the Director of the Office of Management and Budget, the Chairman of the Council of Economic Advisors, the Assistant to the President for National Security Affairs, the Assistant to the President for Economic Policy, and the Assistant to the President for Homeland Security and Counterterrorism. The President can also appoint temporary members to the Committee as he determines.

Cases

In addition to the Dubai Ports cases, a number of investment transactions have attracted public and Congressional attention. After a lengthy review by CFIUS in 2000, Verio, Inc., a U.S. firm that operates websites for businesses and provides internet services, was acquired by NTT Communications of Japan. Verio's stock price reportedly fell during the CFIUS investigation as a result of uncertainty in the market about prospects for the transaction. The CFIUS review was instigated by the FBI, which had expressed concerns during the initial review stage that the majority interest of the Japanese government in NTT could give it access to information regarding wiretaps that were being conducted on email and other Web-based traffic crossing Verio's computer system. After completing its investigation, however, CFIUS did not recommend that President Clinton block the transaction.

The potentially negative publicity that can be associated with a CFIUS investigation of a transaction apparently has had a major impact on the transactions CFIUS has investigated. Since 1990, nearly half of the transactions CFIUS investigated were terminated by the firms involved, because the firms decided to withdraw from the transactions rather than face a negative determination by CFIUS. In 2006, for instance, the prospect of a CFIUS investigation apparently was the major reason the Israeli firm Check Point Software Technologies decided to call off its proposed $225 million acquisition of Sourcefire, a U.S. firm specializing in security appliances for protecting a corporation's internal computer networks. In addition, the decision by the China National Offshore Oil Company (CNOOC) to drop its proposed $18 billion acquisition of Unocal oil company in 2005 was partly due to concerns by CNOOC about an impending CFIUS investigation of the transaction.

In 2009, Brazilian food producer JBS agreed to pay $800 million to acquire a majority stake in Texas chicken company Pilgrim's Pride Corp., which was undergoing a bankruptcy reorganization plan. The Brazilian firm is among the world's largest meat producers; it is a major beef producer and distributor with dairy and leather industries. In a separate case, CFIUS reportedly agreed in 2013 to the pending acquisition of Sprint Nextel for $20 billion by the Japanese firm SoftBank. One complication with the transaction was that Sprint had agreed to acquire Clearwire for $2.2 billion. Clearwire, however, relied on the Chinese firm Huawei for equipment and for cell tower base stations. SoftBank agreed to remove Huawei as a supplier when the acquisition of Sprint is finalized. DISH Network reportedly made a counter offer of $25.5 billion that Sprint was considering.

Between December 2009 and July 2010, two Chinese firms withdrew their proposed acquisitions of U.S. firms due to opposition from at least one CFIUS agency. In December 2009, the Chinese firm Northwest Nonferrous International Investment Corp., a subsidiary of China's largest aluminum producer, attempted to acquire U.S.-based Firstgold. The transactions was withdrawn by the Chinese firm due to objections by the U.S. Department of the Treasury that Firstgold had properties near sensitive military bases. In June 2010, China's Tangshan Caofedian Investment Corporation withdrew its proposed acquisition of Emcore, which makes components for fiber optics and solar panels, due to "regulatory concerns."[32] In September 2012, the Chinese firm Dalian Wanda Group acquired AMC Entertainment for $2.6 billion. AMC is the owner and operator of over 338 movie theaters in the United States. With the purchase, the Chinese firm became the largest theater owner in the world.

In 2012, two investments by Chinese firms attracted public and congressional attention: an investment by the Chinese firm Sany Group in a wind farm project, known as the Butter Creek Projects, in Oregon by Ralls Corp.; and Wanxiang's acquisition of battery-maker A123 Systems Inc. In March 2012, Ralls acquired the wind farm assets from Terna Energy SA, an Athens, Greece-based company, without reporting the transaction to CFIUS. In June, 2012, CFIUs contacted Ralls and requested the firm file a voluntary notification to have its investment retroactively reviewed. After reviewing the acquisition, CFIUS recommended that Ralls stop operations until a complete investigation could be completed as a result of objections by the U.S. Navy over the placement of wind turbines by Ralls near or within restricted Naval Weapons Systems Training Facility airspace where drones (unmanned aerial vehicles) are tested. After a full investigation, CFIUS recommended that President Obama block the investment by ordering a divestment of the transaction and imposed other requirements on Ralls to remove equipment it had installed.

On September 28, 2012, President Obama issued an executive order[33] that argued that there was credible evidence that the Ralls acquisition threatened to impair U.S. national security and ordered Ralls to divest itself of the Oregon wind farm project. In response, the Ralls Corporation filed a suit on October 1, 2012 challenging the Obama Administration's authority to block the investment. On February 22, 2013, the United States District Court for the District of Columbia dismissed the suit by ruling that the court lacked jurisdiction, since the CFIUS statute states that the President's decisions are not subject to judicial review, known as a finality provision.[34] Ralls argued that the President was authorized only to "suspend of prohibit" a transaction, not to order a removal of equipment or a divesture.

The court ruled, however that the statute grants the President broad authority by authorizing him to take "such action for such time" as he considers appropriate. The suit also argued that Ralls was treated unfairly under the Due Process Clause of the Fifth Amendment, but the court ruled that it lacked jurisdiction on this motion as well by the CFIUS statute. Nevertheless, the court indicated that its ruling would not prohibit Ralls' due process claim to proceed. The Ralls' due process claim apparently focused on whether the President and/or CFIUS should be required to provide companies that proceed through the CFIUS review and investigation process with an opportunity to review, respond to, and rebut any evidence used to make a Presidential Determination. One issue involved in requiring access to such information is the fact that CFIUS' analysis for any particular transaction is based on classified information that generally is not available to the public. Ralls has appealed the case.

In another case, China's Wanxiang Group received approval in January 2013 from CFIUS to acquire electric car battery maker A123 Systems. Wanxiang outbid other potential buyers by offering to pay $257 million for the U.S. company. Some Members of Congress and the Strategic Materials Advisory Council argued against the acquisitions on the grounds that it could jeopardize the nation's energy security. Others opposed the acquisition because A123 Systems had received nearly $250 million in a federal grant to support clean energy, although half of the grant was never released. A123 Systems manufactures lithium-ion batteries for Fisker Automotive, BMW hybrid 3- and 5-series cars, and the all-electric Chevrolet Spark.

The proposed 2013 acquisition of Smithfield Food Inc., for $4.7 billion by China's Shuanghui International Holdings Ltd., potentially the largest acquisition of a U.S. firm by a Chinese company, sparked intense Congressional and public interest about the issue of food security as a component of the critical infrastructure/key resources rubric. Smithfield Foods is the world's leading vertically integrated pork processor and pork producer. It is the leading U.S. pork packer and producer, capturing about 26% share of the domestic U.S. hog market and produces around 20-22 million hogs per year, compared with the Chinese market that slaughtered nearly 694 million hogs in 2012. The Smithfield operation spans facilities including hog farms, pork processing and packing, and pork distribution facilities in more than a dozen states, including North Carolina, Virginia, Maryland, South Dakota, Ohio, Iowa, Illinois, Nebraska, Indiana, Kansas, Minnesota, Missouri, Kentucky, and Wisconsin. Opposition to the proposed acquisition was expressed by the National Farmers Union and the Center for Rural Affairs due to concerns over the impact on market concentration. In addition, the proposed acquisition of Smithfield Foods could challenge state laws that bar foreign ownership of farmland in Iowa, Missouri, and other Midwest states, given Smithfield's wide-spread operations. Some observers called for CFIIUS to appoint the Secretary of Agriculture as a temporary member of CFIUS to review the proposed transaction. Another issue involved in the transaction is that Smithfield has developed and uses advanced genetic research to produce especially lean pigs that may well be desired by Shuanghui and potentially could raise questions about the protection of Smithfield's intellectual property and future competition.

The Smithfield-Shuanghui acquisition also raises questions about the implications for U.S. critical infrastructure/key resources associated with this particular investment transaction, but also about U.S. food security over the long-term and whether such concerns are being addressed sufficiently during a CFIUIS review or investigation. According to this argument, since Smithfield Foods is a vertically integrated company, its acquisition potentially could affect a number of different markets and different parts of the food production infrastructure, but the acquisition potentially provides a future competitor with the necessary resources to mount a competitive challenge in the future to other U.S. food producers. The National Strategy for Critical Infrastructures and Key Assets, adopted in the wake of the 2001 terrorist attacks, identifies the critical infrastructure nature of the food and agriculture sector as, "the fundamental need for food, as well as great public sensitivity to food safety makes assuring the security of food production and processing a high priority."[35] The strategy defines the food and agriculture sector as: 1) the supply chains for feed, animals, and animal products; 2) crop production and the supply chains of seed, fertilizer, and other necessary related materials; and 3) the post-harvesting components of the food supply chain, from processing, production, and packaging through storage and distribution to retail sales, institutional food services, and restaurant or home consumption.

The growing number of investments by Chinese firms has raised concerns by a number of groups over the economic and security impact of the investments, similar to concerns about Japanese investment in the United States in the 1980s. In particular, on October 8, 2012, the House Permanent Select Committee on Intelligence published a report[36] on the "the counterintelligence and security threat posed by Chinese telecommunications companies doing business in the United States." The report offered a number of policy recommendations affecting CFIUS, including:

- The Committee on Foreign Investment in the United States (CFIUS) must block acquisitions, takeovers, or mergers involving Huawei and ZTE given the threat to U.S. national security interests. Legislative proposals seeking to expand CFIUS to include purchasing agreements should receive thorough consideration by relevant Congressional committees.
- Committees of jurisdiction in the U.S. Congress should consider potential legislation to better address the risk posed by telecommunications companies with nation-state ties or otherwise not clearly trusted to build critical infrastructure. Such legislation could include increasing information sharing among private sector entities, and an expanded role for the CFIUS process to include purchasing agreements.

In addition, in November 2012, the U.S.-China Economic and Security Review Commission[37] issued a report that detailed concerns over Chinese investments by U.S. industries, lawmakers, and government officials about the ‘‘potential economic distortions and national security concerns arising from China's system of state-supported and state-led economic growth." In particular, some observers argued that economic concerns focused on the possibility that state-backed Chinese companies choose to invest ‘‘based on strategic rather than market-based considerations,'' and are free from the constraints of market forces because of generous state subsidies. The report proffered a number of recommendations for amending the CFIUS statute:

- Congress examine foreign direct investment from China to the United States and assess whether there is a need to amend the underlying statute (50 U.S.C. app 2170) for the Committee on Foreign Investment in the United States (CFIUS) to (1) require a mandatory review of all controlling transactions by Chinese state- owned and state-controlled companies investing in the United States; (2) add a net economic benefit test to the existing national security test that CFIUS administers; and (3) prohibit investment in a U.S. industry by a foreign company whose government prohibits foreign investment in that same industry.
- Legislation creating the Committee on Foreign Investment in the United States (CFIUS) could be amended to add a test of ''economic benefit'' of a Chinese investment in the United States.
- CFIUS's jurisdiction be extended to include ''greenfield'' investments, or investments in new industrial plants and facilities.

Covered Transactions

The law requires CFIUS to review all "covered" foreign investment transactions to determine whether a transaction threatens to impair the national security, or the foreign entity is controlled by a foreign government, or it would result in control of any "critical infrastructure that could impair the national security." A covered foreign investment transaction is defined as any merger, acquisition, or takeover which results in "foreign control of any person engaged in interstate commerce in the United States." According to Treasury Department regulations, investment transactions that are *not* considered to be covered transactions under the Exon-Florio provision and, therefore, not subject to a CFIUS review are those that are undertaken "solely for the purpose of investment, " or an investment in which the foreign investor has "no intention of determining or directing the basic business decisions of the issuer." In addition, investments that are solely for investment purposes are defined as those (1) in which the transaction does not involve owning more than 10% of the voting securities of the firm; or (2) those investments that are undertaken directly by a bank, trust company, insurance company, investment company, pension fund, employee benefit plan, mutual fund, finance company, or brokerage company "in the ordinary course of business for its own account."[38] Other transactions that are not covered include (1) stock splits or pro rata stock dividend that does not involve a change in control; (2) an acquisition of any part of an entity or of assets that do not constitute a U.S. business; (3) an acquisition of securities by a person acting as a securities underwriter, in the ordinary course of business and in the process of underwriting; and an acquisition pursuant to a condition in a contract of insurance relating to fidelity, surety, or casualty obligations if the contract was made by an insurer in the ordinary course of business. In addition, the Treasury regulations also stipulate that the extension of a loan or a similar financing arrangement by a foreign person to a U.S. business will not be considered a covered transaction and will not be investigated, unless the loan conveys a right to the profits of the U.S. business or involves a transfer of management decisions.

Critical Infrastructure

A new element to the CFIUS process that was added by P.L. 110-49 is the addition of "critical industries" and "homeland security" as broad categories of economic activity that could be subject to a CFIUS national security review. After the September 11th terrorist attacks Congress passed and President Bush signed the USA PATRIOT Act of 2001 (Uniting and Strengthening America by Providing Appropriate Tools Required to Intercept and Obstruct Terrorism).[39] In this act, Congress provided for special support for "critical industries," which it defined as:

> systems and assets, whether physical or virtual, so vital to the United States that the incapacity or destruction of such systems and assets would have a debilitating impact on security, national economic security, national public health or safety, or any combination of those matters.[40]

This broad definition is enhanced to some degree by other provisions of the act, which identify certain sectors of the economy that are likely candidates for consideration as components of the national critical infrastructure. These sectors include telecommunications, energy, financial services, water, transportation sectors,[41] and the "cyber and physical infrastructure services critical to maintaining the national defense, continuity of government, economic prosperity, and quality of life in the United States."[42] The following year, Congress adopted the language in the Patriot Act on critical infrastructure into The Homeland Security Act of 2002.[43]

In addition, the Homeland Security Act added key resources to the list of critical infrastructure (CI/KR) and defined those resources as: "publicly or privately controlled resources essential to the minimal operations of the economy and government."[44] Through a series of Directives, the Department of Homeland Security identified 17 sectors[45] of the economy as falling within the definition of critical infrastructure/key resources and assigned primary responsibility for those sectors to various Federal departments and agencies, which are designated as Sector-Specific Agencies (SSAs).[46] On March 3, 2008, Homeland Security Secretary Chertoff signed an internal DHS memo designating Critical Manufacturing as the 18th sector on the CI/KR list.

Control

The statute itself does not provide a definition of the term "control," but such a definition is included in the Treasury Department's regulations. According to those regulations, control is not defined as a numerical benchmark,[47] but instead focuses on a functional definition of control, or a definition that is governed by the influence the level of ownership permits the foreign entity to affect certain decisions by the firm. According to the Treasury Department's regulations:

> The term control means the power, direct or indirect, whether or not exercised, and whether or not exercised or exercisable through the ownership of a majority or a dominant minority of the total outstanding voting securities of an issuer, or by proxy voting, contractual arrangements or other means, to determine, direct or decide matters affecting an entity; in particular, but without limitation, to determine, direct, take, reach or cause decisions regarding:
>
> (1) The sale, lease, mortgage, pledge or other transfer of any or all of the principal assets of the entity, whether or not in the ordinary course of business;
> (2) The reorganization, merger, or dissolution of the entity;
> (3) The closing , relocation, or substantial alternation of the production operational, or research and development facilities of the entity;
> (4) Major expenditures or investments, issuances of equity or debt, or dividend payments by this entity, or approval of the operating budget of the entity;

(5) The selection of new business lines or ventures that the entity will pursue;
(6) The entry into termination or non-fulfillment by the entity of significant contracts;
(7) The policies or procedures of the entity governing the treatment of non-public technical, financial, or other proprietary information of the entity;
(8) The appointment or dismissal of officers or senior managers;
(9) The appointment or dismissal of employees with access to sensitive technology or classified U.S. Government information; or
(10) The amendment of the Articles of Incorporation, constituent agreement, or other organizational documents of the entity with respect to the matters described at paragraph (a) (1) through (9) of this section.

The Treasury Department's regulations also provide some guidance to firms that are deciding whether they should notify CFIUS of a proposed or pending merger, acquisition, or takeover. The guidance states that proposed acquisitions that need to notify CFIUS are those that involve "products or key technologies essential to the U.S. defense industrial base." This notice is not intended for firms that produce goods or services with no special relation to national security, especially toys and games, food products, hotels and restaurants, or legal services. CFIUS has indicated that in order to assure an unimpeded inflow of foreign investment it would implement the statute "only insofar as necessary to protect the national security," and "in a manner fully consistent with the international obligations of the United States."[48]

Neither Congress nor the Administration has attempted to define the term national security. Treasury Department officials have indicated, however, that during a review or investigation each CFIUS member is expected to apply that definition of national security that is consistent with the representative agency's specific legislative mandate.[49] The concept of national security was broadened by P.L. 110-49 to include, "those issues relating to 'homeland security,' including its application to critical infrastructure."

Procedures

According to the amended Exon-Florio provision, the President or any member of CFIUS can initiate a review of an investment transaction in addition to a review that is initiated by the parties to a transaction providing a formal notification. As amended, CFIUS has 30 days to review a transaction to decide after it receives the initial formal notification by the parties to a merger, acquisition, or a takeover, whether to investigate a case as a result of its determination that the investment "threatens to impair the national security of the United States." National security also includes "those issues relating to 'homeland security,' including its application to critical infrastructure," and "critical technologies." In addition, CFIUS is required to conduct an investigation of a transaction if the Committee determines that the transaction would result in foreign control of any person engaged in interstate commerce in the United States. During such a review, the members of CFIUS are also required to consider the 12 factors that Congress has authored as a basis for assessing the impact of the investment. If during this 30-day period all of the members of CFIUS conclude that the investment does not threaten to impair the national security, the review is terminated. If, however, at least one member of the Committee determines that the investment does threaten to impair the national security CFIUS can proceed to a 45-day investigation.

During the 30-day review stage, the Director of National Intelligence, although not a member of CFIUS, is required to carry out a thorough analysis of "any threat to the national security of the United States" of any merger, acquisition, or takeover. This analysis is required to be completed "within 20 days" of the receipt of a notification by CFIUS, but the statute directs that the DNI must be given "adequate time," presumably if this national security review cannot be completed within the 20-day requirement This analysis would include a request for information from the Department of the Treasury's Director of the Office of Foreign Assets Control and the Director of the Financial Crimes Enforcement Network. In addition, the Director of National Intelligence is required to seek and to incorporate the views of "all affected or appropriate" intelligence agencies.

CFIUS is also required to review "covered" investment transactions in which the foreign entity is owned or controlled by a foreign government, but the law provides an exception to this requirement. A review is exempted if the Secretary of the Treasury and certain other specified officials determine that the transaction in question will not impair the national security. It is somewhat unclear, however, how this requirement will mesh with the established process. The measure does not amend or alter the current statute in the area that has been the source of differences between CFIUS and Congress.

Presidential Authority

As previously indicated, P.L. 110-49 grants the President the authority to block proposed or pending foreign "mergers, acquisitions, or takeovers" of "persons engaged in interstate commerce in the United States" that threaten to impair the national security. Congress directed that before this authority can be invoked the President must conclude that (1) other U.S. laws are inadequate or inappropriate to protect the national security; and (2) that he must have "credible evidence" that the foreign investment will impair the national security. As a result, if CFIUS determines, as was the case in the Dubai Ports transaction, that it does not have credible evidence that an investment will impair the national security, then it argues that it is not required to undertake a full 45-day investigation, even if the foreign entity is owned or controlled by a foreign government. After considering the two conditions listed above (other laws are inadequate or inappropriate, and he has credible evidence that a foreign transaction will impair national security), the President is granted almost unlimited authority to take "*such action for such time as the President considers appropriate to suspend or prohibit any covered transaction that threatens to impair the national security of the United States*." In addition, such determinations by the President are not subject to judicial review, as was emphasized in the ruling by the U.S. District Court for the District of Columbia in the case of Ralls vs. the Committee on Foreign Investment in the United States.

In addition, the President, acting through CFIUS, is required to conduct a National Security investigation and to take any "necessary" actions as part of the 45-day investigation if the review indicates that at least one of three conditions exists. These three conditions are (1) as a result of a review of the transaction, CFIUS determines that the transactions threaten to impair the national security of the United States and that the threat had not been mitigated during or prior to a review of the transaction; (2) the foreign person is controlled by a foreign government; or (3) the transactions would result in the control of any critical infrastructure by a foreign person, the transactions could impair the national security, and that such impairment had not been mitigated. At the conclusion of the investigation or the 45-day review period, whichever comes first, the Committee can decide to offer no recommendation or it can recommend that the President suspend or prohibit the investment. The President is under no obligation to follow the recommendation of the Committee to suspend or prohibit an investment.

During a review or an investigation, CFIUS and a designated lead agency have the authority to negotiate, impose, or enforce any agreement or condition with the parties to a transaction in order to mitigate any threat to the national security of the United States. Such agreements are to be based on a "risk-based analysis" of the threat posed by the transaction. Also, if a notification of a transaction is withdrawn before any review or investigation by CFIUS can be completed, the amended law grants the Committee the authority to take a number of actions. In particular, the Committee could develop (1) interim protections to address specific concerns about the transaction pending a re-submission of a notice by the parties; (2) specific time frames for re-submitting the notice; and (3) a process for tracking any actions taken by any parties to the transaction.

Factors for Consideration

The Exon-Florio provision includes a list of 12 factors the President must consider in deciding to block a foreign acquisition. These factors are also considered by the individual members of CFIUS as part of their own review process to determine if a particular transaction threatens to impair the national security. This list includes the following elements:

(1) domestic production needed for projected national defense requirements;
(2) the capability and capacity of domestic industries to meet national defense requirements, including the availability of human resources, products, technology, materials, and other supplies and services;
(3) the control of domestic industries and commercial activity by foreign citizens as it affects the capability and capacity of the U.S. to meet the requirements of national security;
(4) the potential effects of the transactions on the sales of military goods, equipment, or technology to a country that supports terrorism or proliferates missile technology or chemical and biological weapons; and transactions identified by the Secretary of Defense as "posing a regional military threat" to the interests of the United States;
(5) the potential effects of the transaction on U.S. technological leadership in areas affecting U.S. national security;
(6) whether the transaction has a security-related impact on critical infrastructure in the United States:
(7) the potential effects on United States critical infrastructure, including major energy assets;

(8) the potential effects on United States critical technologies;
(9) whether the transaction is a foreign government-controlled transaction;
(10) in those cases involving a government-controlled transaction, a review of (A) the adherence of the foreign country to nonproliferation control regimes, (B) the foreign country's record on cooperating in counter-terrorism efforts, (C) the potential for transshipment or diversion of technologies with military applications,;
(11) the long-term projection of the United States requirements for sources of energy and other critical resources and materials; and
(12) such other factors as the President or the Committee determine to be appropriate.[50]

Factors 6-12 that were added through P.L. 110-49 potentially broaden significantly the scope of CFIUS's reviews and investigations. Previously, CFIUS had been directed by Treasury Department regulations to focus its activities primarily on investments that had an impact on U.S. national defense security. The additional factors, however, incorporate economic considerations into the Exon-Florio process in a way that was specifically rejected when the measure initially was adopted and refocuses CFIUS's reviews and investigations to consider the broader rubric of economic security. In particular, CFIUS is now required to consider the impact of an investment on critical infrastructure as a factor for considering recommending that the President block or postpone a transaction. Critical infrastructure is defined in broad terms within the measure as "any systems and assets, whether physical or cyber-based, so vital to the United States that the degradation or destruction of such systems or assets would have a debilitating impact on national security, including national economic security and national public health or safety."

As originally drafted, the Exon-Florio provision also would have applied to joint ventures and licensing agreements in addition to mergers, acquisitions, and takeovers. Joint ventures and licensing agreements subsequently were dropped from the proposal because the Reagan Administration and various industry groups argued at the time that such business practices were deemed to be beneficial arrangements for U.S. companies. In addition, they argued that any potential threat to national security could be addressed by the Export Administration Act[51] and the Arms Control Export Act.[52]

Confidentiality Requirements

The Exon-Florio provision also codified confidentiality requirements that are similar to those that appeared in Executive Order 11858 by stating that any information or documentary material filed under the provision may not be made public "except as may be relevant to any administrative or judicial action or proceeding."[53] The provision does state, however, that this confidentiality provision "shall not be construed to prevent disclosure to either House of Congress or to any duly authorized committee or subcommittee of the Congress." The provision provides for the release of proprietary information "which can be associated with a particular party" to committees only with assurances that the information will remain confidential. Members of Congress and their staff members will be accountable under current provisions of law governing the release of certain types of information. The Exon-Florio provision requires the President to provide a written report to the Secretary of the Senate and the Clerk of the House detailing his decision and his actions relevant to any transaction that was subject to a 45-day investigation.[54]

Mitigation and Tracking

Since the implementation of the Exon-Florio provision in the 1980s, CFIUS had developed several informal practices that likely were not envisioned when the statute was drafted. In particular, members of CFIUS on occasion had negotiated conditions with firms to mitigate or to remove business arrangement that raised national security concerns among the members of CFIUS. Such agreements often were informal arrangements that had an uncertain basis in statute and had not been tested in court. These arrangements often were negotiated during the formal 30- day review period, or even during an informal process prior to the formal filing of a notice of an investment transaction.

According to P.L. 110-49, CFIUS must designate a lead agency to negotiate, modify, monitor, and enforce agreements in order to mitigate any threat to national security. Such agreements are required to be based on a "risk-based analysis" of the threat posed by the transaction. CFIUS is also required to develop a method for evaluating the compliance of firms that have entered into a mitigation agreement or condition that was imposed as a requirement for approval of the investment transaction. Such measures, however, are required to be developed in such a way that they allow CFIUS to determine that compliance is taking place without also (1) "unnecessarily diverting" CFIUS resources from assessing any new covered transaction for which a written notice had been filed; and (2) placing "unnecessary" burdens on a party to a investment transaction.

On February 20, 2008, Bain Capital and Huawei Technologies withdrew their offer to acquire the network and software firm 3Com for $2.2 billion, due to an inability to successfully negotiate a mitigation agreement with members of CFIUS. Bain Capital is a privately held asset management and investment firm, and Huawei Technologies is the largest networking and telecommunications equipment supplier in China. 3Com is a publicly held company that specializes in networking equipment and in the Tipping Point network intrusion prevention software. Such software is used by various U.S. defense firms to prevent outside groups from accessing their confidential databases. Bain Capital and Huawei reportedly withdrew their proposal after they failed to agree to terms with CFIUS over a mitigation agreement and stated that they would restructure the deal and resubmit it at a later date in 2008.[55]

If a notification of a transaction is withdrawn before any review or investigation by CFIUS can be completed, CFIUS can take a number of actions, including (1) interim protections to address specific concerns about the transaction pending a re-submission of a notice by the parties; (2) specific time frames for resubmitting the notice; and (3) a process for tracking any actions taken by any party to the transaction. Also, any federal entity or entities that are involved in any mitigation agreement are to report to CFIUS if there is any modification that is made to any agreement or condition that had been imposed and to ensure that "any significant" modification is reported to the Director of National Intelligence and to any other federal department or agency that "may have a material interest in such modification." Such reports are required to be filed with the Attorney General.

Congressional Oversight

P.L. 110-49 significantly increases the types and number of reports that CFIUS is required to send to certain specified Members of Congress. In particular, CFIUS is required to brief certain congressional leaders if they request such a briefing and to report annually to Congress on any reviews or investigations that it had conducted during the prior year. Each report must include a list of all reviews and investigations that had been conducted, information on the nature of the business activities of the parties involved in an investment transaction, information about the status of the review or investigation, and information on any withdrawal from the process, any roll call votes by the Committee, any extension of time for any investigation, and any presidential decision or action taken under the Exon-Florio provision. In addition, CFIUS is required to report on trend information on the number of filings, investigations, withdrawals, and presidential decisions or actions that were taken. The report must include cumulative information on the business sectors involved in filings and the countries from which the investments originated; information on the status of the investments of companies that withdrew notices and the types of security arrangements and conditions CFIUS used to mitigate national security concerns; the methods the Committee used to determine that firms were complying with mitigation agreements or conditions; and a detailed discussion of all perceived adverse effects of investment transactions on the national security or critical infrastructure of the United States.

The Secretary of the Treasury, in consultation with the Secretary of State and the Secretary of Commerce, is required to conduct a study on investment in the United States, particularly in critical infrastructure and industries affecting national security by (1) foreign governments, entities controlled by or acting on behalf of a foreign government, or persons of foreign countries which comply with any boycott of Israel; or (2) foreign governments, entities controlled by or acting on behalf of a foreign government, or persons of foreign countries which do not ban organizations designated by the Secretary of State as foreign terrorist organizations. In addition, CFIUS is required to provide an annual evaluation of any credible evidence of a coordinated strategy by one or more countries or companies to acquire U.S. companies involved in research, development, or production of critical technologies in which the United States is a leading producer. The report must include an evaluation of possible industrial espionage activities directed or directly assisted by foreign governments against private U.S. companies aimed at obtaining commercial secrets related to critical technologies.

The Inspector General of the Department of the Treasury is required to investigate any failure of CFIUS to comply with requirements for reporting that were imposed prior to the passage of P.L. 110-49 and to report the findings of this report to Congress. In particular, the report must be sent to the chairman and ranking Member of each committee of the House and the Senate with jurisdiction over any aspect of the report, including the Committee on Foreign Relations, the Committee on Foreign Affairs, the Committee on

Financial Services, and the Committee on Energy and Commerce of the House.

The chief executive officer of any party to a merger, acquisition, or takeover is required to certify in writing that the information contained in the written notification to CFIUS fully complies with the requirements of the Exon-Florio provision and that the information is accurate and complete. This written notification would also include any mitigation agreement or condition that was part of a CFIUS approval.

CFIUS SINCE EXON-FLORIO

Recent information indicates that the number of mergers and acquisitions fell in 2008 and 2009, as indicated in **Table 1**. Although the number of successful investment transactions rebounded in 2010 and 2011, they lag behind the large number of transactions that occurred in 2006 and 2007. The decline in the number of successful mergers and acquisitions in 2008 and 2009 likely resulted from the financial crisis during that period in which access to capital was sharply curtailed. Based on the number of transactions per year, acquisitions of U.S. firms by other U.S. firms have accounted for the largest share of all merger and acquisition (M&A) transactions over the past 15 years. This share fell from 73% of all U.S. M&A transactions in 2003 to 66% in 2011, down from the 68.5% share recorded in the previous year. The share of M&A activity attributed to foreign firms acquiring U.S. firms in 2011 accounted for 14.2% of all such transactions, up from 13.7% in the previous year. In addition, U.S. firms acquiring foreign firms also increased in 2011, accounting for 20% of the total number of transactions, up from 17.8% recorded in 2010.

Table 1. Merger and Acquisition Activity in the United States, 1996-2011

	Total Number of Mergers and Acquisitions	U.S. Firms Acquiring U.S. Firms	Non-U.S. Firms Acquiring U.S. Firms	U.S. Firms Acquiring Non-U.S. Firms
1996	7,347	5,585	628	1,134
1997	8,479	6,317	775	1,387
1998	10,193	7,575	971	1,647
1999	9,173	6,449	1,148	1,576

	Total Number of Mergers and Acquisitions	U.S. Firms Acquiring U.S. Firms	Non-U.S. Firms Acquiring U.S. Firms	U.S. Firms Acquiring Non-U.S. Firms
2000	8,853	6,032	1,264	1,557
2001	6,296	4,269	923	1,104
2002	5,497	3,989	700	808
2003	5,959	4,357	722	880
2004	7,031	5,084	813	1,134
2005	7,600	5,463	977	1,160
2006	8,621	6,105	1,142	1,374
2007	9,477	6,505	1,408	1,564
2008	7,626	5,172	1,127	1,327
2009	5,862	4,099	815	948
2010	7,309	5,006	1,004	1,299
2011	7,413	4,875	1,055	1,483

Source: *Mergers & Acquisitions*, February 2012.

Table 2. Foreign Investment Transactions Reviewed by CFIUS, 2008-2010

Year	Number of Notices	Notices Withdrawn During Review	Number of Investigations	Notices Withdrawn During Investigation	Presidential Decisions
2008	155	18	23	5	0
2009	65	5	25	2	0
2010	93	6	35	6	0
Total	313	29	93	13	0

Source: *Annual Report to Congress*, Committee on Foreign Investment in the United States, December 2011.

Recent Transactions

According to the annual report filed by CFIUS under the requirements of P.L. 110-49,[56] CFIUS activity dropped sharply in 2009 and 2010 as a result of tight credit markets willing to fund acquisitions and takeovers during the global financial crisis, but rebounded in 2010, as indicated in **Table 2**. During the three-year period 2008-2010, foreign investors sent 313 notices to CFIUS of plans to acquire, takeover, or merge with a U.S. firm. Of the investment transactions that were notified, about 10% were withdrawn during the initial 30-day review; about 30% of the total transactions that were notified were determined to require a 45-day investigation. Also, of the transactions that were investigated, about 14% were withdrawn before a final determination could be reached. As a result, of the 313 proposed investment transactions that were notified to CFIUS, 261 transactions, or 83% of the transactions were completed. The CFIUS report also indicates that a presidential decision was not made in any of the transactions, whether because transactions that might have been recommended by CFIUS be blocked by the President were withdrawn before CFIUS could make its recommendation, or because CFIUS did not offer a recommendation that a transaction be blocked by the President.

The CFIUS report also indicates that three-fourths of the foreign investment transactions that were notified to CFIUS were in the manufacturing and finance, information, and services sectors, as indicated in Error! Reference source not found. Within the manufacturing sector, about half of all the investment transactions notified to CFIUS were in the computer and electronic products sectors. The next two sectors with the highest number of transactions were the transportation equipment sector and the machinery sector. Investment transactions in the services sector accounted for two-thirds of the total number of investment transactions in the finance, information, and services category.

Table 4 shows foreign investment transactions by the home country of the foreign investor and the industry composition of the investment transactions. According to data based on notices provided to CFIUS by foreign investors, British investors were the most active in acquisitions, takeovers, or mergers during the 2008-2010 period, accounting for nearly one-third of the total number of transactions. France and Israel join the United Kingdom as the top three countries of origin for investors providing notifications to CFIUS. In all three countries, investments were concentrated in the manufacturing and finance, information, and services sectors. The ranking of countries in **Table 4** differs in a number of important ways from data published by the Bureau of Economic Analysis on the cumulative amount, or the total book value, of foreign direct investment in the United States, which places the United Kingdom, Japan, Netherlands, Germany, Canada, and Switzerland as the most active countries of origin for foreign investment in the United States.

Table 3. Industry Composition of Foreign Investment Transactions Reviewed by CFIUS, 2008-2010

Year	Manufacturing	Finance, Information, and Services	Mining, Utilities, and Construction	Wholesale and Retail Trade	Total
2008	72	42	25	16	155
2009	21	22	19	3	65
2010	36	35	13	9	93
Total	129	99	57	28	313

Source: *Annual Report to Congress*, Committee on Foreign Investment in the United States, December 2011.

Table 4. Country of Foreign Investor and Industry Reviewed by CFIUS, 2008-2010

Year	Manufac-turing	Finance, Information, and Services	Mining, Utilities, and Construction	Wholesale and Retail Trade	Total
United Kingdom	44	37	8	2	91
France	14	4	4	3	25
Israel	13	9		2	24
Canada	3	9	10	2	24
Japan	4	8	6	1	19
China	8	3	4	1	16
Russian Fed.	6	3	2	1	12
Italy	8	2			10
Netherlands	2	4	1	1	8
Sweden	3	5			8
Total	**129**	**99**	**57**	**28**	**313**

Source: *Annual Report to Congress*, Committee on Foreign Investment in the United States, December 2011.

The CFIUS annual report also provides some general information on the total number of cases in which it applied legally binding mitigation measures. The report did not list any specific cases or measures, but it did indicate that CFIUS applied mitigation measures to 16 cases in the 2008-2010 period. According to CFIUS, in 2010, CFIUS agencies negotiated, and parties adopted, mitigation measures for nine covered transactions.[57] Mitigation measures have included a number of different approaches, including

- Requiring a subsidiary with sensitive technology or classified contracts have a separate and independent board of directors composed of U.S. citizens.
- Requiring the board of directors to establish a security committee composed of independent directors who are U.S. citizens and have independent authority over security compliance.
- Restricting the type of information that can be provided by the U.S. subsidiary to the foreign parent and the identity/number of parent company employees who are allowed access to the information.
- Restricting access by non-U.S. citizens to critical infrastructure.
- Requiring the screening of employees and contractor personnel with access to critical infrastructure.
- Requiring firms to obtain prior approval of seller contracts for certain goods or services where the seller is foreign-owned.
- Requiring firms adopt and implement network and IT security policy.

CFIUS also has implemented procedures to evaluate and ensure that parties to a investment transaction remain in compliance with any risk mitigation measures that were adopted to gain approval of the investment.

As a consequence of the confidential nature of the CFIUS review of any proposed transaction, there are few official sources of information other than the congressionally mandated annual report concerning the Committee's work. For the most part, information concerning individual transactions that have been reviewed by CFIUS or any final recommendations that have been issued by CFIUS have come from announcements released by the companies involved in a transaction and not by CFIUS. According to one source,[58] CFIUS had received more than 1,500 notifications between 1988 and 2006, of which it conducted a full investigation of 25 cases. Of these 25 cases, 13 transactions were withdrawn upon notice that CFIUS would conduct a full review and 12 of the remaining transactions cases were sent to the President. Of these 12 transactions, 1 was prohibited.[59]

IMPACT OF THE EXON-FLORIO PROCESS ON CFIUS

The DP World case exposed a number of important aspects of CFIUS's operations that apparently were not well known or understood by the public in general. Many of these concerns were addressed in P.L. 110-49. As already indicated, the Exon-Florio provision stipulates a three-step process: the formal notification to CFIUS and a 30-day review; a 45-day investigation for those transactions that raised national security concerns during the 30-day review and for those in which the concerns were not resolved during the review period; and a 15-day presidential determination stage for those transactions that were determined after the 45-day review to pose an impairment to national security. Over time, however, this process apparently evolved to include an informal fourth stage of unspecified length of time that consists of an unofficial CFIUS determination prior to the formal filing with CFIUS. This type of informal review developed because it likely has served the interests of both CFIUS and the firms involved in an investment transaction. According to Treasury Department officials, this informal contact enables "CFIUS staff to identify potential issues before the review process formally begins."[60] This informal process is likely to continue under the provisions of P.L. 110-49. An important difference, however, is that CFIUS gained legislative authority under P.L. 110-49 to negotiate and enforce agreements with foreign investors to mitigate the effects of an investment transaction on national security.

For CFIUS members, the informal process has been beneficial because it has given them as much time as they have felt was necessary to review a transaction without facing the time constraints that arise under the formal CFIUS review process. This informal review likely has also given the CFIUS members added time to negotiate with the firms involved in a transaction to restructure the transaction in ways that have addressed any potential security concerns or to develop other types of conditions that members of CFIUS feel are appropriate in order to remove security concerns.

The DP World acquisition demonstrated how this informal CFIUS process operates in reviewing a proposed foreign investment transaction. According to officials involved in the review, DP World officials contacted the Treasury Department in early October 2005 to informally discuss their proposed transaction. Treasury officials directed DP World to consult with the Department of Homeland Security and in November the Treasury officials requested an intelligence assessment from the Director of National Intelligence. Staff representatives from all of the CFIUS members met on December 6, 2005, to discuss the transaction, apparently to determine if there were any security concerns that had not been addressed and resolved during the two-month-long informal review of the proposed transaction.

Ten days after that meeting, DP World filed its official notification with CFIUS, which distributed the notification to all of the CFIUS members and to the Departments of Energy and Transportation. During this process, the Department of Homeland Security apparently negotiated a letter of assurances with DP World that addressed some outstanding concerns about port security. On the basis of this letter and the lack of any remaining concerns expressed by any member of CFIUS or other agencies that were consulted, CFIUS completed its review of the transaction on January 17, 2006, and concluded that the transaction did not threaten to impair the national security and therefore that it did not warrant a 45-day investigation.[61]

CONCLUSION

On July 26, 2007, President Bush signed P.L. 110-49, the Foreign Investment and National Security Act of 2007. The Treasury Department released its regulations implementing this law on November 21, 2008, as the global financial crisis was the focus of attention. In 2008, tight credit conditions associated with the global financial crisis and the slowdown in the rate of growth in the U.S. economy retarded merger and acquisition activities in the United States and abroad. There has been no particular foreign acquisition that has provoked a public backlash comparable to some acquisitions that occurred prior to the financial crisis. On June 20, 2011, the Obama Administration issued a formal statement on foreign investment declaring the countries' commitment to an open investment policy.[62] Some in Congress and elsewhere are dissatisfied, however, that the legislation in its present form does not address a broad range of issues concerning foreign investment. For instance, when the measure was debated and approved, the extent and nature of sovereign wealth funds (SWFs) in which entities controlled by foreign governments invest in U.S. firms was relatively unknown. In addition, the sub-prime mortgage crisis was just emerging and foreign investors had not yet taken substantial stakes in prominent U.S. financial firms. These investments are challenging some established notions of the role of foreign investment in the economy and the concept of what role economic issues play within the rubric of national security.

These and other concerns about foreign investment underscore the significant differences that remained between Congress and the Bush

Administration over the operations of CFIUS and over the economic and security objectives the Committee should pursue. The proposed acquisition of P&O by Dubai Ports World sparked a broader set of concerns and a wide-ranging discussion between Congress and the Bush Administration over a working set of parameters that establishes a functional definition of the national economic security implications of foreign direct investment. In part, this issue reflects differing assessments of the economic impact of foreign investment on the U.S. economy and differing political and philosophical convictions among Members and between Congress and the Administration.

The incident also focused attention on the informal process firms use to have their investment transactions reviewed by CFIUS prior to a formal review. According to anecdotal evidence, some firms apparently believe that the CFIUS process is not market neutral, but that it adds to market uncertainty that can negatively affect a firm's stock price and lead to economic behavior by some firms that is not optimal for the economy as a whole. Such behavior might involve firms expending a considerable amount of resources to avoid a CFIUS investigation, or deciding to terminate a transaction that would improve the optimal performance of the economy in order to avoid a CFIUS investigation. While such anecdotal evidence does not provide enough evidence to serve as the basis for developing public policy, it does raise a number of concerns about the possible impact of the CFIUS process on the market and the potential costs of redefining the concept of national security relative to foreign investment.

The focus by Congress on the Committee has also shown that the DP World transaction, in combination with other recent unpopular foreign investment transactions, exacerbated dissatisfaction among some Members of Congress over the operations of CFIUS. In particular, some Members were displeased with the discretionary authority the Committee used under the Exon-Florio provision to investigate certain foreign investment transactions. As a result, Congress changed the process to require more frequent contacts between the Committee, which generally operates without much public or congressional attention, and Congress. Congress also expanded its oversight role over the Committee.

The DP World transaction also revealed that the September 11, 2001, terrorist attacks fundamentally altered the viewpoint of some Members of Congress regarding the role of foreign investment in the economy and over the impact of such investment on the national security framework. These observers argued that this change in perspective required a reassessment of the role of foreign investment in the economy and of the implications of corporate ownership of activities that fall under the rubric of critical infrastructure. As a result, Congress amended the CFIUS process to enhance Congress's oversight role while it reduced somewhat the discretion of CFIUS to review and investigate foreign investment transactions in order to have CFIUS investigate a larger number of foreign investment cases. In addition, the DP World transaction focused attention on long-unresolved issues concerning the role of foreign investment in the nation's overall security framework and the methods that are being used to assess the impact of foreign investment on the nation's defense industrial base, critical infrastructure, and homeland security.

In 2012, the growing number of investments by Chinese firms sparked concerns by a number of groups over the economic and security impact of the investments, similar to concerns about Japanese investment in the United States in the 1980s. In particular, on October 8, 2012, the House Permanent Select Committee on Intelligence published a report[63] on the "the counterintelligence and security threat posed by Chinese telecommunications companies doing business in the United States." The report offered a number of policy recommendations affecting CFIUS, including

- The Committee on Foreign Investment in the United States (CFIUS) must block acquisitions, takeovers, or mergers involving Huawei and ZTE given the threat to U.S. national security interests. Legislative proposals seeking to expand CFIUS to include purchasing agreements should receive thorough consideration by relevant Congressional committees.
- Committees of jurisdiction in the U.S. Congress should consider potential legislation to better address the risk posed by telecommunications companies with nation-state ties or otherwise not clearly trusted to build critical infrastructure. Such legislation could include increasing information sharing among private sector entities, and an expanded role for the CFIUS process to include purchasing agreements.

In addition, in November 2012, the U.S.-China Economic and Security Review Commission[64] issued a report that detailed concerns over Chinese investments by U.S. industries, lawmakers, and government officials about the "potential economic distortions and national security concerns arising from China's system of state-supported and state-led economic growth." In particular, some observers argued that economic concerns focused on the possibility that state-backed Chinese companies choose to invest "based on strategic rather than market-based considerations,'' and are free from the constraints of market forces because of generous state subsidies. The report proffered a number of recommendations for amending the CFIUS statute:

- Congress examine foreign direct investment from China to the United States and assess whether there is a need to amend the underlying statute (50 U.S.C. app 2170) for the Committee on Foreign Investment in the United States (CFIUS) to (1) require a mandatory review of all controlling transactions by Chinese state- owned and state-controlled companies investing in the United States; (2) add a net economic benefit test to the existing national security test that CFIUS administers; and (3) prohibit investment in a U.S. industry by a foreign company whose government prohibits foreign investment in that same industry.
- Legislation creating the Committee on Foreign Investment in the United States (CFIUS) could be amended to add a test of ''economic benefit'' of a Chinese investment in the United States.
- CFIUS's jurisdiction be extended to include ''greenfield'' investments, or investments in new industrial plants and facilities.

Most economists agree that there is little economic evidence to conclude that foreign ownership, whether by a private entity or by an entity that is owned or controlled by a foreign government, has a measurable impact on the U.S. economy. Others may argue that such firms pose a risk to national security or to homeland security, but such concerns are not within the purview of this report. Similar issues concerning corporate ownership were raised during the late 1980s and early 1990s when foreign investment in the U.S. economy increased rapidly. There are little new data, however, to alter the conclusion reached at that time that there is no definitive way to assess the economic impact of foreign ownership or of foreign investment on the economy. Although some observers have expressed concerns about foreign investors who are owned or controlled by foreign governments acquiring U.S. firms, there is little confirmed evidence that such a distinction in corporate ownership has any effect on the economy as whole.

For most economists, the distinction between domestic- and foreign-owned firms, whether the foreign firms are privately owned or controlled by a foreign government, is sufficiently small that they would argue that it does not warrant placing restrictions on the inflow of foreign investment. Nevertheless, foreign direct investment does entail various economic costs and benefits. On the benefit side, such investments bring added capital into the economy and potentially could add to productivity growth and innovation. Such investment also represents one repercussion of the U.S. trade deficit. The deficit transfers dollar-denominated assets to foreign investors, who then decide how to hold those assets by choosing among various investment vehicles, including direct investment. Foreign investment also removes a stream of monetary benefits from the economy in the form of repatriated capital and profits that reduces the total amount of capital in the economy. Such costs and benefits likely occur whether the foreign owner is a private entity or a foreign government.

End Notes

[1] Executive Order 11858 (b), May 7, 1975, 40 F.R. 20263.

[2] U.S. Congress. House. Committee on Government Operations. Subcommittee on Commerce, Consumer, and Monetary Affairs. *The Operations of Federal Agencies in Monitoring, Reporting on, and Analyzing Foreign Investments in the United States*. Hearings. 96th Cong., 1st sess., Part 3, July 30, 1979. Washington: GPO, 1979. p. 334-335. (Hereinafter cited as, *The Operations of Federal Agencies*, part 3.)

[3] Peninsular and Oriental Steam Company is a leading ports operator and transport company with operations in ports, ferries, and property development. It operates container terminals and logistics operations in over 100 ports and has a presence in 18 countries.

[4] Dubai Ports World was created in November 2005 by integrating Dubai Ports Authority and Dubai Ports International. It is one of the largest commercial port operators in the world with operations in the Middle East, India, Europe, Asia, Latin America, the Caribbean, and North America.

[5] Weisman, Jonathan, and Bradley Graham, "Dubai Firm to Sell U.S. Port Operations," *The Washington Post*, March 10, 2006. p. A1.

[6] King, Neil Jr., and Greg Hitt, Dubai Ports World Sells U.S. Assets—AIG Buys Operations that Ignited Controversy As Democrats Plan Changes. *The Wall Street Journal*, December 12, 2006. p. A1.

[7] The term "representative" was dropped by Executive Order 12661, December 27, 1988, 54 FR 780.

[8] Executive Order 11858 (b), May 7, 1975, 40 F.R. 20263.

[9] P.L. 94-472, Oct 11, 1976; 22 USC 3101.

[10] P.L. 94-472, Oct 11, 1976; 22 USC Section 3101(b).

[11] U.S. Congress. House. Committee on Government Operations. *The Adequacy of the Federal Response to Foreign Investment in the United States*. Report by the Committee on Government Operations. H.Rept. 96-1216, 96th Cong., 2nd sess., Washington: GPO, 1980. 166-184.

[12] *The Operations of Federal Agencies*, part 3, p. 5.

[13] U.S. Congress. House. Committee on Energy and Commerce. Subcommittee on Commerce, Consumer Protection, and Competitiveness. *Foreign Takeovers and National Security*. Hearings on Section 905 of H.R. 3. 100th Cong., 1st sess., October 20, 1987. Testimony of David C. Mulford. Washington: GPO, 1988. p. 21-22.

[14] P.L. 100-418, Title V, Section 5021, August 23, 1988; 50 USC Appendix sect. 2170.

[15] Auerbach, Stuart. Cabinet to Weigh Sale of Chip Firm. *The Washington Post*, March 12, 1987. p. E1.

[16] Sanger, David E. Japanese Purchase of Chip Maker Canceled After Objections in U.S. *The New York Times*, March 17, 1987. p. 1.

[17] Pollack, Andrew. Schlumberger Accepts Offer. *The New York Times*, September 1, 1987. p. D1.

[18] Kilborn, Peter T. Curb Asked On Foreign Takeovers. *The New York Times*, March 18, 1987. p. D1.

[19] P.L. 100-418.

[20] Testimony of Patrick A. Mulloy before the Committee on Banking, Housing, & Urban Affairs, October 20, 2005.

[21] Auerbach, Stuart. "President Tells China to Sell Seattle Firm." *The Washington Post*, February 8, 1990, p. A1; and Benham, Barbara. "Blocked Takeover Fuels Foreign Policy Flap." *Investor's Daily*, February 8, 1990. p. 1.

[22] CRS Report RL33103, *Foreign Investment in the United States: Major Federal Statutory Restrictions*, by Michael V. Seitzinger.

[23] Executive Order 12661 of December 27, 1988, 54 F.R. 779.

[24] Regulations Pertaining to Mergers, Acquisitions, and Takeovers by Foreign Persons. 31 C.F.R. Part 800.

[25] 31 CFR Part 800, November 21, 2008.

[26] P.L. 102-484, October 23, 1992.

[27] Briefing on the Dubai Ports World Deal before the Senate Armed Services Committee, February 23, 2006.

[28] Kirchgaessner, Stephanie, US Threat to Reopen Terms of Lucent and Alcatel Deal Mergers, *Financial Times*, December 1, 2006. P. 19; Pelofsky, Jeremy, Businesses Object to US move on foreign Investment, *Reuters News*, December 5, 2006.

[29] Testimony of Robert Kimmett, Briefing on the Dubai Ports World Deal Before the Senate Armed Services Committee, February 23, 2006.

[30] The United States Trade Representative and the Director of the Office of Science and Technology Policy were added through E.O. 13456, issued January 23, 2008.

[31] Executive Order 11858 of May 7, 1975, 40 F.R. 20263 established the Committee with six members: the Secretaries of State, the Treasury, Defense, Commerce, and the Assistant to the President for Economic Affairs, and the Executive Director of the Council on International Economic Policy. Executive Order 12188, January 2, 1980, 45 F.R. 969, added the United States Trade Representative and substituted the Chairman of the Council of Economic Advisors for the Executive Director of the Council on International Economic Policy. Executive Order 12661, December 27, 1988, 54 F.R. 779, added the Attorney General and the Director of the Office of Management and Budget. Executive Order 12860, September 3, 1993, 58 F.R. 47201, added the Director of the Office of Science and Technology Policy, the Assistant to the President for National Security Affairs, and the Assistant to the President for Economic Policy. Executive Order 13286, Section 57, February 28, 2003, added the Secretary of Homeland Security. P.L. 110-49 reduced the membership of CFIUS to six Cabinet members and the Attorney General, it added the Secretary of Labor and the Director of National Security as ex officio members, and removed seven White House appointees.

[32] Kirchgaessner, Stephanie, US Blocks China Fibre Optics Deal Over Security, *Financial Times*, June 30, 2010.

[33] Order Signed by the President Regarding the Acquisition of Four U.S. Wind Farm Project Companies by Ralls Corporation, The White House, September 28, 2012. Available at http://www.whitehouse.gov/the-press-office/2012/ 09/28/order-signed-president-regarding-acquisition-four-us-wind-farm-project-c.

[34] Ralls Corporation vs. Committee on Foreign Investment in the United States, et al., Civil Action Number 12-1513; available at https://ecf.dcd.uscourts.gov/cgi-bin/show_public_doc ?2012cv1513-46.

[35] *The National Strategy for the Physical Protection of Critical Infrastructure and Key Assets*, February 2003, p. 36.

[36] Investigative Report on the U.S. National Security Issues Posed by Chinese Telecommunications Companies Huawei and ZTE: A Report by Chairman Mike Rogers and Ranking Member C.A. Dutch Ruppersberger of the Permanent Select Committee on Intelligence, U.S. House of Representatives, October 8, 2012.

[37] 2012 Report to Congress of the U.S.-China Economic and Security Review Commission, U.S. China Economic and Security Review Commission, November 2012.

[38] 31 CFR 800.302.

[39] P.L. 107-56, Title X, §1014, October 26, 2001; 42 U.S.C. §5195c(e).

[40] Ibid.

[41] 42 U.S.C. §5195c(b)(2).

[42] 42 U.S.C. §5195c(b)(3).

[43] 6 U.S.C. §101(4).

[44] 6 USC, Sec 101(9).

[45] The sectors include 1) Agriculture and Food; 2) Defense Industrial Base; 3) Energy; 4) Public Health and Healthcare; 5) National Monuments and Icons; 6) Banking and Finance; 7) Drinking Water and Water Treatment Systems; 8) Chemical; 9) Commercial Facilities; 10) Dams; 11) Emergency Services; 12) Commercial Nuclear Reactors, Materials, and Waste; 13) Information Technology; 14) Telecommunications; 15) Postal and Shipping; 16) Transportation Systems; and 17) Government Facilities.

[46] Sector-Specific Agencies include the Departments of: Agriculture, Defense, Energy, Health and Human Services, Homeland Security, Interior, Treasury, and the Environmental Protection Agency.

[47] There are other statutes that do use numerical benchmarks. According to section 13(d) of the Securities Exchange Act of 1934 (15 U.S.C. Section 78m(d) any person who acquires 5% or more of the publicly traded securities of a U.S. firm must report the acquisition of the shares to the Securities and Exchange Commission. For statistical purposes, the United States defines foreign direct investment as the ownership or control, directly or indirectly, by one foreign person (individual, branch, partnership, association, government, etc.) of 10% or more of the voting securities of an incorporated U.S. business enterprise or an equivalent interest in an unincorporated U.S. business enterprise 15 CFR §806.15 (a)(1). This level of ownership requires foreign owners to file quarterly and longer annual reports with the Department of Commerce as part of the quarterly and annual reports on the balance of payments and gross domestic product (GDP).

[48] Ibid.

[49] Senate Armed Services Committee, Briefing on the Dubai Ports World Ports Deal, February 23, 2006.

[50] The last requirement under factor 4 and factors 6-12 were added by P.L. 110-49.

[51] 50 U.S.C. App. Section 2401, as amended.

[52] 22 U.S.C. App. 2778 et seq.

[53] 50 U.S.C. Appendix Section 2170(c)

[54] 50 U.S.C. Appendix Section 2170(g).

[55] US Insiders Point to Bain Errors Over 3Com, *The Financial Times Limited*, March 3, 2008.

[56] *Annual Report to Congress*, Committee on Foreign Investment in the United States, December 2011.

[57] *Annual Report to Congress*, Committee on Foreign Investment in the United States, December 2011

[58] CFIUS, *The Washington Post*, July 3, 2005. p. F3.

[59] Auerbach, Stuart. "President Tells China to Sell Seattle Firm." *The Washington Post*, February 3, 1990. p. A1; and Benham, Barbara. "Blocked Takeover Fuels Foreign Policy Flap." *Investor's Daily*, February 8, 1990. p. 1.

[60] Testimony of Robert Kimmett, Briefing on the Dubai Ports World Deal before the Senate Armed Services Committee, February 23, 2006.

[61] Ibid.

[62] Statement by the President on United States Commitment to Open Investment Policy, the White House, June 20, 2011.

[63] Investigative Report on the U.S. National Security Issues Posed by Chinese Telecommunications Companies Huawei and ZTE: A Report by Chairman Mike Rogers and Ranking Member C.A. Dutch Ruppersberger of the Permanent Select Committee on Intelligence, U.S. House of Representatives, October 8, 2012.

[64] 2012 Report to Congress of the U.S.-China Economic and Security Review Commission, U.S. China Economic and Security Review Commission, November 2012.

INDEX

#

112th Congress, x, 82
20th century, 32

A

ability, viii, ix, 6, 29, 33, 38, 49, 51, 61, 72, 73, 74, 81, 83
access, 4, 37, 44, 65, 87, 90, 92, 94, 100, 108, 112
accountability, 58, 59, 60
accounting, 8, 13, 15, 108, 110
acquisitions, viii, 18, 19, 20, 21, 26, 42, 56, 58, 64, 65, 71, 73, 86, 88, 89, 91, 93, 94, 96, 100, 102, 104, 108, 109, 110, 114, 116
adjustment, 16
Administration, ix, x, 5, 7, 39, 50, 65, 68, 71, 77, 82, 84, 86, 87, 89, 90, 94, 100, 104, 114, 115
adverse effects, 107
Africa, 23, 53, 54
age, viii, 25, 30
agencies, ix, 36, 44, 60, 62, 66, 81, 85, 88, 99, 101, 111, 114
agriculture, 96
Air Force, 69
Alexander Hamilton, 31
alters, 83
ambassadors, 34
American, viii, 3, 5, 10, 29, 31, 32, 34, 41, 44, 46, 53, 83
American Bar Association, 46
anecdotal evidence, x, 82, 115
annihilation, 77
antitrust, viii, 30, 87
antitrust laws, viii, 30
appointees, 119
Argentina, 79
armed forces, 39
Asia, 23, 53, 54, 80, 118
assessing the costs and benefits, ix, 50
assessment, 62, 72, 76, 77, 113
assets, 1, 10, 24, 26, 55, 61, 66, 78, 83, 93, 98, 99, 103, 104, 118
attitudes, 66, 87
Attorney General, 41, 92, 106, 119
Austria, 22
authority, x, 33, 34, 35, 36, 43, 44, 45, 64, 65, 71, 82, 85, 86, 87, 88, 91, 94, 102, 103, 112, 115
automobiles, 80
average earnings, 10

B

backlash, 114
balance of payments, 11, 26, 78, 79, 120
ban, 107

bank charter, 42
bank holding companies, 2, 8
banking, 2, 9, 16, 19, 20, 21, 31, 38, 42, 43, 52, 64, 88
banking sector, 20
bankruptcy, 93
banks, 31, 32, 43
barriers, 38, 59, 72
base, 6, 63, 65, 70, 93, 100, 116
batteries, 95
BEA, 10, 11, 37
beef, 93
Belgium, 15, 22
benchmarks, 120
beneficiaries, 75
benefits, ix, 3, 15, 24, 26, 35, 50, 51, 60, 63, 64, 71, 72, 73, 74, 75, 76, 77, 78, 117
BHC, 42, 43
biological weapons, 103
block a Chinese acquisition, x, 82
bonds, 31, 83
Brazil, 2, 4, 8, 79
Britain, 20
broader, viii, ix, 25, 49, 50, 61, 67, 104, 115
Bureau of Labor Statistics, 37
business cycle, 6
business environment, 64
businesses, vii, viii, 1, 3, 5, 13, 16, 17, 18, 29, 32, 34, 38, 51, 53, 64, 68, 86, 92
businesses and real estate, vii, viii, 17, 18, 29, 51, 53
buyers, 94

C

Cabinet, 118, 119
canals, 31
candidates, 98
capital accumulation, 72
capital inflow, 58, 75
cargoes, 39
Caribbean, 80, 118
categorization, 16
caveats, x, 82
Census, 16, 37
certificate, 39, 40
certification, 35
CFR, vii, 17, 79, 119, 120
challenges, 68
characterizes, viii, 30, 71
chemical(s), 8, 103
chicken, 93
Chief Justice, 30
Chile, 79
China, 2, 4, 8, 16, 54, 68, 79, 87, 93, 94, 95, 96, 97, 106, 111, 116, 117, 119, 120, 121
Chinese firms, 93, 96, 116
chromium, 70
cities, 40
citizens, 31, 32, 38, 39, 40, 41, 44, 45, 75, 103, 112
citizenship, 33, 34, 35, 38, 39, 40, 41
civil service, 35
classes, 65
classification, 34, 35
clean energy, 95
climate, vii, 1, 31, 87
coal, 2, 8, 40
cobalt, 70
colleges, 2, 4, 15
commerce, 16, 30, 33, 44, 45, 64, 65, 86, 89, 97, 101, 102
commercial, ix, 31, 35, 45, 63, 80, 81, 83, 87, 103, 107, 118
Committee on Foreign Investment, v, ix, 44, 45, 48, 65, 80, 81, 82, 85, 96, 97, 102, 109, 111, 116, 117, 119, 120
communication, 61
communism, 36
community, 2, 5, 15, 61, 64
compensation, 10, 24, 55
competition, 95
competitive advantage, 63
competitiveness, 5, 68
competitors, 73
compliance, 16, 105, 112
composition, 64, 110
computer, 85, 86, 92, 110
Concise, 46
confidentiality, 59, 105

congressional, viii, x, 29, 32, 37, 66, 82, 83, 85, 89, 93, 106, 115
consensus, ix, 50
consent, 78, 80, 90
consistent, x, 45, 55, 59, 65, 82, 100
Constitution, 32, 34
constitutional duties, x, 82
constitutional limitations, viii, 30
construction, 21, 40, 44
consumer markets, 4
consumers, 5
consumption, 96
context, ix, 3, 50, 58, 61, 76, 77
Continental, 31, 40
contributes, viii, 29, 64
controversial, 90
copper, 70
cost, 5, 16, 19, 20, 26, 44, 50, 51, 71, 72, 73, 74, 75, 76, 78, 79
cost saving, 5
cost-benefit analysis, 71, 72
country, viii, 4, 6, 13, 29, 34, 38, 39, 40, 41, 42, 46, 57, 63, 64, 68, 71, 74, 76, 77, 87, 103, 104, 110
country of origin, 4, 71
covering, 57
credit market, 109
creditor nation, 32, 46
creditworthiness, 31
critical infrastructure, 60, 61, 62, 66, 67, 74, 95, 96, 97, 98, 99, 100, 101, 102, 103, 104, 107, 112, 116
criticism, 32, 83
crop, 96
crop production, 96

D

danger, 77
data availability, 16
data set, 11
debtor nation, 46
debts, 23, 31
deficit, 118
deflate, 19, 52
degradation, 104
deliberations, x, 82
Department of Commerce, v, vii, 1, 7, 9, 11, 12, 13, 14, 16, 17, 18, 19, 20, 21, 23, 26, 37, 51, 52, 53, 78, 120
Department of Defense, 44, 65, 69, 85
Department of Energy, 7, 44
Department of Homeland Security, 66, 99, 113, 114
Department of the Treasury, 101, 107
deposits, 40
depth, 62
destruction, 61, 66, 74, 76, 77, 98, 104
detail, viii, 30
developing countries, 54
DHS, 66, 99
direct cost, 73
direct investment(s), vii, viii, ix, x, 11, 15, 16, 17, 18, 19, 20, 21, 24, 25, 26, 36, 49, 50, 51, 52, 53, 54, 57, 58, 63, 64, 67, 68, 69, 78, 82, 83, 85, 87, 88, 118
directors, 32, 38, 39, 42, 112
disclosure, x, 23, 36, 37, 38, 41, 66, 82, 105
discrimination, 59
dispersion, 75, 78
disposition, 34, 40
dissatisfaction, 115
distortions, 96, 116
distribution, 53, 64, 95, 96
District of Columbia, 39, 45, 94, 102
domestic investment, 46, 59
domination, viii, 29
Dubai Ports World, ix, 66, 67, 68, 77, 80, 81, 83, 89, 115, 118, 119, 120, 121
due process, 94

E

earnings, 19, 26, 53, 78, 79
economic activity, viii, 49, 50, 71, 98
economic damage, 61
economic development, 8, 50
economic downturn, 15
economic efficiency, 71

economic growth, 6, 20, 26, 52, 54, 59, 96, 116
economic impact, ix, 50, 71, 77, 87, 115, 117
economic incentives, 72
economic performance, 77
economic power, 86
economic theory, 72
economic well-being, 61
economics, 16, 35
Egypt, 79
election, 32, 42
electricity, 6
emergency, 33
emerging markets, 8, 15
empirical studies, 16
employee compensation, 24, 55
employees, 100, 112
employers, 24
employment, 2, 10, 15, 21, 24, 35, 59, 64
energy, vii, x, 1, 2, 3, 4, 5, 6, 7, 15, 64, 66, 82, 94, 98, 103, 104
energy security, 94
England, 30, 31
environment, vii, ix, 1, 3, 6, 49, 57, 58, 64, 87
Environmental Protection Agency, 80, 120
equipment, 6, 8, 10, 24, 93, 94, 103, 106, 110
equitable, x, 68, 82
equity, 19, 23, 26, 38, 78, 99
equivalent, vii, 17, 19, 76, 79, 120
espionage, 107
Estonia, 79
Europe, 22, 31, 32, 53, 80, 118
European Union, 53, 63
evaluating, ix, 50, 75, 105
evidence, x, 6, 37, 82, 86, 94, 102, 107, 115, 117
evil, 30
exclusion, 30, 56
executive branch, ix, x, 81, 82, 84
Executive Order, x, 65, 78, 80, 82, 83, 84, 85, 88, 90, 91, 105, 118, 119
exercise, ix, 30, 33, 45, 81, 83
expedient, x, 82
expenditures, 13, 16, 99
expertise, 8, 60
export control, 65
exports, 3, 6, 10, 12, 15, 46
extensively, ix, 50
extraction, 6

F

fair, x, 68, 82
fairness, 60
faith, 34
farmland, viii, 29, 95
farms, 95
FBI, 92
FDI, vii, 1, 2, 3, 4, 6, 8, 13, 15, 16
FDI inflow, 2, 7, 8
federal executive branch, ix, 81
federal government, 32, 33, 35, 36, 38, 40, 42, 44, 47
Federal Government, 36
federal law, 35
Federal Reserve, 42, 43
Federal Reserve Board, 43
fell, vii, 10, 17, 19, 53, 87, 92, 108
fiber, 93
fiber optics, 93
fidelity, 98
Fifth Amendment, 94
financial, x, 8, 9, 11, 16, 26, 43, 54, 66, 78, 82, 98, 100, 108, 110, 114
Financial Crimes Enforcement Network, 101
financial firms, 114
financial markets, x, 82
financial resources, 8
fishing, 35
food, 93, 95, 100
food production, 95
food products, 100
food safety, 96
food security, 95
food services, 96
force, 35

Ford, 83, 84, 85
foreign affairs, x, 82
foreign banks, 13, 14
foreign companies, vii, 1, 2, 3
foreign direct investment, vii, viii, ix, 1, 3, 10, 11, 16, 17, 18, 19, 20, 21, 24, 26, 36, 37, 49, 50, 51, 52, 53, 54, 57, 58, 63, 67, 69, 71, 76, 77, 78, 83, 85, 86, 87, 97, 110, 115, 117, 120
foreign exchange, 8, 68
foreign firms, 10, 15, 19, 21, 24, 25, 54, 65, 71, 108, 117
foreign governments, x, 36, 37, 42, 55, 58, 67, 68, 72, 77, 82, 83, 84, 85, 107, 114, 117
foreign money, viii, 29
foreign nationals, 34
foreign ownership, viii, 10, 16, 29, 30, 38, 41, 64, 95, 117
foreign person, vii, 17, 30, 37, 45, 98, 102, 120
formation, 64
Fourteenth Amendment, 34, 35, 46
France, 13, 15, 20, 22, 58, 79, 86, 110, 111
free trade, 57
freedom, 59
full employment, 72
funding, 3
funds, x, 10, 19, 23, 41, 54, 56, 68, 72, 82, 83, 114

G

GDP, 5, 7, 16, 24, 120
Germany, 13, 15, 20, 22, 58, 61, 79, 110
global economy, viii, 15, 49, 50, 68
global recession, 6, 7, 16
globalization, viii, 26, 30, 49, 50
globe, vii, 1
goods and services, 6, 55, 75
governments, x, 36, 37, 42, 55, 57, 58, 61, 67, 68, 72, 77, 82, 83, 84, 85, 107, 114, 117
grants, 39, 64, 86, 94, 102, 103
grazing, 41
Greece, 79, 93
gross domestic product, 24, 120
growth, 6, 7, 13, 16, 19, 24, 26, 54, 64, 68, 72, 114
growth rate, 72
guidance, 59, 84, 87, 100
guidelines, 59, 77, 87

H

harvesting, 96
health, 61
Health and Human Services, 80, 120
history, viii, 30, 32
holding company, 16, 42, 43
home and abroad, x, 64, 82
homeland security, 66, 67, 74, 98, 100, 101, 116, 117
Homeland Security Act, 66, 99
Hong Kong, 16
host, 15, 63, 64, 79
hotels, 100
House, x, 78, 80, 82, 87, 90, 96, 105, 107, 116, 118, 120, 121
House of Representatives, 120, 121
household income, 5
human, 103
human resources, 103
hybrid, 95

I

identification, 71
identity, 112
immigration, viii, 30, 32, 35
immigration laws, viii, 30
impact assessment, 60
impair, viii, x, 30, 33, 64, 65, 68, 82, 86, 94, 97, 101, 102, 103, 114
implemented, x, 51, 78, 82, 88, 91, 112
implementing, x, 43, 78, 80, 82, 88, 90, 114
imports, 15, 46
income, 19
independence, 31, 33
India, 4, 79, 80, 118

indirectly, vii, 17, 36, 41, 78, 85, 120
individuals, 41, 78
Indonesia, 79
industrial sectors, 20, 64
industries, viii, 6, 8, 21, 22, 23, 24, 25, 29, 32, 38, 45, 66, 69, 75, 86, 87, 93, 96, 98, 103, 107, 116
industry, 4, 5, 8, 9, 10, 16, 31, 37, 38, 39, 55, 73, 97, 104, 110, 117
inflation, 5, 26
informal practices, 105
information sharing, 96, 116
information technology, 61
infrastructure, 2, 4, 6, 15, 58, 60, 62, 64, 66, 67, 90, 95, 98, 99, 104, 116
initiatives, ix, 50
integration, 64
intellectual property, 4, 5, 95
intelligence, 101, 113
interest rates, 26
international competitiveness, 26
international investment, 36, 56, 58, 62, 68, 85
international law, 30, 57
International Monetary Fund, 7, 16
international policies, ix, 49, 50
international trade, 64
intervention, 71, 72, 73, 76
investing abroad, viii, 17, 25
investment by foreigners, viii, 30
investment policy, x, 4, 58, 59, 60, 61, 68, 71, 82, 87, 114
investments, vii, viii, 3, 5, 8, 10, 16, 17, 19, 20, 21, 26, 29, 31, 32, 33, 34, 35, 51, 52, 53, 54, 56, 57, 58, 62, 64, 65, 68, 83, 84, 85, 93, 96, 97, 99, 104, 107, 110, 114, 116, 117, 118
investors, ix, x, 5, 8, 11, 20, 21, 23, 25, 26, 31, 34, 38, 45, 49, 51, 54, 56, 57, 58, 64, 67, 68, 71, 73, 74, 75, 77, 78, 82, 88, 90, 110, 113, 114, 117, 118
Iowa, 32, 48, 95
Ireland, 22
iron, 69, 70
isolationist., viii, 30
Israel, 79, 107, 110, 111
issues, 16, 31, 62, 67, 70, 91, 100, 101, 113, 114, 116, 117
Italy, 22, 79, 111

J

Japan, 2, 8, 13, 20, 23, 54, 79, 86, 92, 110, 111
joint ventures, 104
jurisdiction, 94, 96, 97, 107, 116, 117
justifications, viii, 30

K

key defense, viii, 29
Korea, 2, 23

L

labor force, 2, 4, 15, 24, 72
largest recipient, vii, viii, 1, 3, 49, 50, 54, 68
Latin America, 53, 54, 80, 118
Latvia, 79
laws, viii, 30, 33, 34, 35, 38, 39, 40, 41, 42, 45, 59, 62, 64, 77, 86, 87, 102
laws and regulations, 77
lead, 72, 103, 105, 115
leadership, 46, 103
learning, 3
legal protection, vii, 1, 3
legislation, 32, 84, 88, 96, 114, 116
legislative authority, 113
less favorably, ix, 49, 51
liberal policy, viii, 29
light, 26, 36, 51
linkage, x, 81
lithium, 95
Lithuania, 79
loans, 23, 26, 78
local government, vii, 17, 34
logistics, 80, 118
long-term, ix, 49, 51, 73, 95, 104

M

machinery, 110
magazines, 41
magnetic properties, 80
magnets, 69, 80
majority, 2, 10, 13, 16, 21, 42, 92, 93, 99
management, 34, 42, 83, 98, 106
manganese, 70
manufacturing, 2, 4, 6, 8, 10, 11, 13, 16, 19, 20, 21, 24, 25, 52, 110
marginal costs, 75, 76, 77
market concentration, 95
market share, 25
marketing, 21
Maryland, 95
mass, 41
mass communication, 41
materials, 41, 44, 69, 70, 96, 103, 104
matter, viii, 3, 29
meat, 93
media, 20, 41
median, 5
Medicare, 36
Members, ix, x, 49, 50, 51, 62, 67, 71, 77, 81, 82, 83, 85, 89, 94, 105, 106, 115
membership, 35, 119
mergers, 19, 26, 56, 58, 64, 65, 71, 73, 86, 89, 91, 96, 102, 104, 108, 110, 116
metals, 69, 70, 85
Mexico, 34
Middle East, 80, 118
military, 80, 85, 86, 93, 103, 104
Minneapolis, 48
missions, 4
Missouri, 95
mobile phone, 80
molybdenum, 70
motivation, 87
multinational companies, 10, 55
multinational corporations, 54
multinational firms, 20, 64

N

NAFTA, 34
national and economic security, viii, 18
national borders, viii, 49, 50
National Defense Authorization Act, 69, 89
national emergency, viii, 29, 75, 87
national interests, 84
national parks, 40
national policy, 75
National Strategy, 95, 120
nationality, 34, 35, 62
natural gas, 6, 40
negative, viii, x, 15, 17, 23, 82, 91, 92
negative factor, x, 82
neodymium, 69
net investment, 9
Netherlands, 15, 20, 22, 61, 63, 110, 111
networking, 106
neutral, x, 82, 115
new operations, vii, 1, 3
nickel, 70
noncitizens, 38
non-OECD, 58
North America, 34, 46, 53, 80, 118
North American Free Trade Agreement, 34

O

Obama, x, 82, 84, 94, 114
Obama Administration, x, 82, 84, 94, 114
obscurity, ix, 81, 83
OECD, 34, 54, 56, 57, 58, 59, 60, 62, 77, 79
Office of Management and Budget, 92, 119
officials, 34, 65, 74, 83, 85, 86, 91, 96, 100, 101, 113, 116
oil, 32, 40, 93
open, ix, x, 2, 4, 15, 31, 33, 40, 49, 50, 51, 57, 58, 59, 68, 82, 87, 114
open markets, 50, 59
openness, 68
operating data, 11
operations, vii, ix, 1, 3, 10, 26, 55, 65, 66, 67, 80, 81, 83, 93, 95, 99, 113, 115, 118
opportunities, 6, 34

optimal, x, 82, 115
optimal performance, 115
Organization for Economic Cooperation and Development, 54, 61, 63, 79
output per worker, 25
outsourcing, 58
oversight, ix, 51, 60, 67, 81, 83, 115, 116
ownership, vii, viii, 10, 16, 17, 29, 30, 31, 37, 38, 40, 41, 64, 65, 69, 73, 78, 95, 99, 116, 117, 120

P

pagers, 80
parallel, 65
parents, 23
participants, 77
Patriot Act, 99
pay, viii, 3, 10, 29, 93, 94
peace, 57, 71, 74
perceived, viii, x, 17, 26, 62, 75, 76, 82, 107
performance, x, 16, 24, 77, 82, 115
petroleum, 2, 8, 20, 83
pharmaceuticals, 2, 8
philosophical, ix, 50, 71, 77, 115
phosphate, 40
pigs, 95
plants, 10, 21, 24, 25, 97, 117
police, 35
policy, viii, x, 4, 16, 29, 48, 51, 57, 58, 59, 60, 61, 67, 68, 71, 72, 75, 76, 78, 82, 84, 87, 90, 96, 112, 114, 116
policy issues, 48
policy reform, 16
policymakers, ix, 50, 67, 71, 74, 75, 76
political aspects, 85
political parties, 42
population, 57
portfolio, 36, 83, 84
portfolio investment, 36
positive correlation, 6
potassium, 40
predictability, 58, 59, 60
preliminary, vii, 17, 18, 19
preparation, 84
preparedness, 33
preservation, 57
president, v, ix, x, 1, 3, 4, 6, 36, 39, 44, 64, 65, 66, 67, 68, 70, 78, 80, 81, 82, 83, 84, 85, 86, 87, 88, 89, 90, 91, 92, 94, 98, 100, 102, 103, 104, 105, 110, 112, 114, 119, 120, 121
President Bush, x, 66, 68, 78, 80, 82, 83, 87, 89, 90, 91, 98, 114
President Clinton, 92
President Obama, x, 4, 82, 94
prevention, 106
price deflator, 19, 52
principles, 30, 35, 58, 59
private enterprises, 31
private investment, 2, 12
private sector, 10, 96, 116
procedural right, 47
producers, 93, 95
productive workers, vii, 1, 3
productivity growth, 5, 118
project, 41, 58, 59, 79, 93, 94, 119
propaganda, 42
property, viii, 4, 5, 16, 30, 31, 33, 80, 95, 118
proportionality, 58, 59, 60
proposition, 33, 74
prosperity, 59, 66, 68, 99
protect, viii, 5, 29, 34, 56, 57, 58, 60, 62, 65, 68, 74, 86, 100, 102
protection, 5, 16, 35, 45, 46, 57, 95
protectionism, 51, 59, 71, 75, 77
public concern(s), 26, 87
public health, 57, 61, 66, 98, 104
public interest, 41, 43, 44, 45, 64, 88, 95
public policy, 74, 76, 115
public safety, 61
public service, 64, 88

Q

quality of life, 66, 99

R

R&D investments, 5, 13
race, 35
radio, 41
rate of return, 25
real estate, vii, viii, 17, 18, 19, 21, 24, 29, 31, 51, 52, 53
rebounded, vii, 7, 17, 108, 110
recession, 2, 10
recognition, 4
recommendations, 42, 59, 69, 85, 88, 96, 97, 112, 116, 117
record surpassed, vii, 17
recovery, 2, 10
reexamination, ix, 49
reflects, ix, 50, 52, 53, 54, 77, 87, 115
Reform, 90
regulations, 5, 40, 58, 65, 84, 88, 97, 99, 100, 104, 114
reinsurance, 39
renewable energy, 6
repair, 44
reputation, 5
requirements, 33, 37, 39, 45, 60, 67, 91, 94, 103, 104, 105, 107, 108, 109
resale, 31
reserves, 6, 7, 8, 68
resources, 38, 66, 71, 72, 73, 74, 76, 88, 95, 99, 104, 106, 115
response, 58, 73, 94
restaurants, 100
restrictions, vii, viii, ix, 30, 32, 38, 39, 41, 43, 44, 50, 51, 56, 57, 58, 59, 60, 62, 64, 77, 78, 117
retail, 10, 19, 20, 21, 24, 52, 96
rights, 33, 34, 57
risk(s), 4, 5, 25, 39, 60, 67, 70, 96, 103, 105, 112, 116, 117
Romania, 79
rules, 57
Russia, 79

S

safety, 57, 61, 66, 98, 104
savings, 5, 46
scarce resources, 72
school, 35
scope, viii, 30, 59, 87, 104
scrutiny, ix, 34, 35, 76, 81, 83, 89
Secretary of Agriculture, 37, 41, 95
Secretary of Commerce, 37, 84, 107
Secretary of Defense, 69, 103
Secretary of Homeland Security, 119
Secretary of the Treasury, 43, 45, 84, 91, 101, 107
securities, vii, 16, 17, 37, 38, 42, 43, 45, 79, 83, 87, 97, 99, 120
Securities Act of 1933, 45
Securities Exchange Act, 38, 120
security threats, 58, 62, 76
seed, 96
seller, 112
Senate, x, 47, 78, 80, 82, 87, 90, 105, 107, 119, 120, 121
sensitivity, 96
sensors, 80
September 11, 2001, ix, x, 26, 49, 51, 56, 66, 76, 81, 83, 98, 115
services, 13, 19, 21, 24, 36, 43, 52, 57, 61, 63, 66, 92, 98, 100, 103, 110, 112
shareholders, 88
shortage, 61
silicon, 70
skilled workers, 5, 10
social consequences, 61
social interests, ix, 49, 50
social life, 61
social welfare, 35
sodium, 40
software, 106
South Africa, 79
South Dakota, 24, 95
sovereign wealth funds, x, 56, 68, 72, 82, 83, 114
sovereignty, 36
Spain, 79

specialization, 20
spending, 2, 13, 19, 20, 53
Sprint, 93
SSA, 90
stability, 58
staff members, 105
state(s), vii, 17, 24, 30, 31, 32, 33, 34, 35, 38, 39, 40, 42, 43, 44, 45, 56, 57, 58, 61, 68, 94, 95, 96, 97, 100, 105, 116, 117
state laws, 34, 35, 38, 95
state-owned enterprises, 68
statistics, 10, 16
statutes, viii, 30, 32, 36, 37, 38, 41, 44, 47, 69, 120
statutory, vii, viii, 30, 91
statutory authority, 91
steel, 6, 85
stock, 6, 40, 41, 43, 64, 91, 92, 98, 115
stock price, 91, 92, 115
storage, 96
structural barriers, 15
structure, ix, 49, 51, 84
struggling, vii, 17
supervision, 45
supervisor, 42
supplier(s), 3, 44, 86, 93, 106
supply chain, 3, 4, 61, 96
Supreme Court, 33, 34, 35, 36
survival, 57, 76
Sweden, 22, 111
Switzerland, 8, 13, 15, 20, 22, 110

T

Taiwan, 8
takeover, 44, 45, 97, 100, 101, 108, 110
tax laws, viii, 30
taxation, 32
taxes, 55
techniques, 25
technological advances, 64
technologies, 25, 61, 65, 100, 104, 107
technology, x, 58, 64, 65, 73, 82, 86, 87, 100, 103, 112
technology company, x, 82
telecommunications, 66, 96, 98, 106, 116
terminals, 80, 118
territorial, 40, 45
territory, 5, 33, 39, 40, 45, 57
terrorism, 58, 68, 103, 104
terrorist attack(s), ix, x, 26, 49, 51, 56, 66, 67, 76, 81, 83, 95, 98, 115
terrorist organization, 107
textbook, 72
The Homeland Security Act, 99
threats, 58, 62, 64, 74, 76
time constraints, 91, 113
time frame, 103, 106
time periods, 73
titanium, 70
Title I, 48
Title V, 69, 118
toys, 100
trade, 2, 8, 10, 13, 15, 16, 19, 20, 21, 22, 23, 24, 34, 36, 52, 57, 58, 59, 86, 118
trade deficit, 118
trademarks, 5
trade-off, 58
trading partners, 44
training, 5
transactions, 11, 15, 16, 21, 59, 65, 67, 69, 85, 87, 88, 89, 92, 93, 97, 101, 102, 103, 107, 108, 110, 112, 113, 115, 116, 117
transmission, 40, 80
transparency, ix, 58, 59, 81, 83
transport, 62, 80, 118
transportation, 6, 8, 66, 98, 110
transshipment, 104
Treasury, 36, 65, 80, 83, 88, 91, 92, 97, 99, 100, 104, 113, 114, 119, 120
treaties, 5, 34, 56, 57
treatment, viii, 4, 30, 34, 51, 57, 62, 68, 77, 100
tungsten, 70

U

U.S. Department of Commerce, vii, 17, 18, 52
U.S. Department of the Treasury, 93

U.S. economy, viii, ix, x, 2, 5, 15, 19, 20, 24, 26, 49, 50, 55, 74, 81, 86, 114, 115, 117
U.S. policy, 63, 64, 68
UK, 22, 61, 79
underwriting, 16, 98
unincorporated, vii, 17, 40, 79, 120
unitary executive branch, x, 82
United Kingdom, 8, 13, 15, 20, 61, 63, 79, 110, 111
United Nations, 18, 53, 56, 79
universities, 2, 4, 5, 15
USA, 66, 98
USA PATRIOT Act, 66, 98

V

validation, 32
valuation, 26, 54, 78
vanadium, 70
variable factor, 73
vehicles, 94, 118
vote, 42, 78, 80, 90
voting, vii, 17, 37, 39, 42, 43, 79, 97, 99, 120
voting securities, vii, 17, 37, 42, 43, 79, 97, 99, 120
vulnerable, viii, 29

W

wages, 3, 5, 8, 10, 24, 25
waiver, 44
war, 30, 74, 76
War on Terror, 74
Washington, 16, 118, 119, 120
waste, 10
waste management, 10
water, 30, 40, 66, 98
wealth, x, 56, 68, 72, 82, 83, 114
web, 16
websites, 92
welfare, 35
well-being, 60
Western Europe, 53
White House, 119, 121
wholesale, 2, 8, 10, 13, 16, 19, 20, 21, 24, 52
wind farm, 93, 94
wind turbines, 94
wiretaps, 92
Wisconsin, 95
withdrawal, 107
workers, vii, 1, 3, 10, 54, 68, 73, 76
workforce, 5
World Bank, 6, 16
World War I, 32, 56, 74
worldwide, 8

Z

zirconium, 70